I Think, You Think, We All Think, Differently

Leadership Skills for Millennials & Gen Z

By Greg Buschman, Ph.D.(c)

Published by Strategic Leadership, Tampa, FL
I Think, You Think, We Think, Differently

www.ithinkyouthink.com
www.gregbuschman.com

ISBN 978-1-7340282-0-1 (eBook Kindle)
ISBN 978-1-7340282-7-0 (eBook EPUB)
ISBN 978-1-7340282-1-8 (Paperback)

Library of Congress Cataloging-in-Publication Data: Greg Buschman, Ph.D.(c). I Think, You Think, We All Think, Differently / Greg Buschman, Ph.D.(c) application submitted.

Limit of Liability / Disclaimer of Warranty

Dedication

This book is dedicated to those who will fill the leadership gap as Traditionalists and Baby Boomers retire. My greatest wish for the Millennial and Gen Z generations is that they learn how to lead our society and economy to new heights without all the hang-ups of past generational transitions.

I love working across generational and cultural lines, especially with Millennials and Gen Z. Maybe that's because my children are Millennials and Gen Z. I love them deeply. I don't want them to have to enter a workforce led by leaders who don't get the flow of our modern society.

I want to say thank you to my wife, Debra Buschman, and our children who have encouraged me and shared in the time and financial sacrifices required to complete a doctoral program and write this book.

Greg Buschman, Ph.D.(c)

Table of Contents

Foreword

Ross Kirwin, MBA
VP & Investment Professional

I was on the front end of the millennial generation entering the workforce, and many managers at that time didn't exactly know "what" we were all about. This book gives so much attention to learning about my generation. It's great to see how much research went into this book.

As opposed to being told, "get a job," the section that encourages folks to ask themselves questions to determine what they want to do, was enlightening. How to choose a fulfilling career is not taught or discussed enough. My dad used to joke that whatever industry you started in would most likely be the industry you will be in for your entire career, so pick wisely. However, I've heard other folks say, "get a job to get experience." Asking these questions throughout your career and life, will be helpful. Doing some soul-searching along the way will help keep you from finding yourself stuck in a job or industry you don't like. Asking these questions after significant life events (getting married, having children) could help identify needed changes.

Something else important I learned from the book, is the reasoning behind how older generations have developed their way of thinking. Having a better understanding could have helped me when I asked for my first raise (just because I was there for a year, I thought I "deserved" it). My manager at that time acknowledged my hard work, and that they were pleased with me. He then asked me if I would like him to ask *his* boss if he should give me a raise, even though the company was not doing well at that time. He got his point across without beating me up. I think back and realize he didn't say what he probably wanted to say. If he did, I would have been depressed and had less productivity. The discussion on how and when Millennials should approach conversations with their superiors about advancement and compensation was helpful.

I am very excited to be a part of a generation that values a balanced work/life balance! The workplace, unfortunately, sometimes looks down on that phrase. The book discusses how Millennials can approach this topic in interviews and gives some options on how to use words that other generations will respond to positively. I feel like the minute a Traditionalist or Boomer hears the phrase "work-life balance," they prejudge what is about to be said or discussed, or possibly the person. What Millennials are saying is, "we as Millennials have experienced first-hand, as children and young adults, what happens when work becomes more of a focus than having a healthy personal life."

Lastly, the info to help Millennials who are currently in organizations that are managed in an authoritarian manner by a Boomer or Traditionalist was helpful. Lots of people will benefit from the advice on what to do if their firm continues to be successful with this approach, thereby never seeing a need to change. Do you get out sooner rather than later? If your firm mainly motivates by money, how do leaders learn there are other ways to reward and get intended behavior, beyond money?

Ross

Jenna Lewis de Ruibal
Marketing Project Manager

I've always been fascinated by the people others seem to want to follow. I wondered what their secret was until I eventually dismissed my curiosity and decided the big man upstairs must have just molded them to be natural-born leaders. I had this one particular boss who was such a spectacular leader. Her followers were always motivated to go above and beyond for her, many times without them even realizing it! In the section where Greg teaches about servant-based leadership, I immediately tuned in to some of the primary reasons my former boss had been so successful — she had been implementing these very principles herself! That gave me a lot of hope that leadership CAN be learned. From reading this book, I learned there is something to the adage "leaders aren't born, they're made."

I also found the story illustrations that shed light on our differing generational paradigms and their impact in the workplace to be particularly insightful. As a Millennial who has reported to both Gen X and Boomer bosses, I only wish I had had this book in my hands at those times. The concepts and truths in this book will most assuredly help you communicate across the generational divide, which can only prove useful when having those conversations about career advancement, raises, and other opportunities. Communication and knowing your audience are vital in becoming an effective leader, and this book empowers you to do just that.

Jenna

Brent Sucher, CMP
Marketing Director

All of this is great. Seriously, I learned a lot from the book. From my perspective, one of the most significant issues the book addressed was, "Why any Millennial or Gen Z might even care about leadership in the first place?!" Be it what others think about it, or the way they currently do things.

"Why should I care? And if I do, what now?" The answer is simple; If you understand and apply the book's content in your communications with others, you will unlock the door to promotions, better income, and happiness in your field while gaining the respect of other generations. The book is bigger than any one of us. It helps people see not just generational differences, but also cultural differences, something that Millennials and Gen Z care about profoundly: sensitivity to identity! Different generations, by default, don't engage on a personal level. Understanding people's personalities and management styles is like acquiring the ability to speak another language. The book's real-life examples and contexts are priceless, "context is power."

One of my most eye-opening takeaways from this book was seeing the side-by-side comparisons of how each generation might handle the same problem or situation, and then discuss how each other generation should manage them. If we as a generation are going to strive to be catalysts of change, to create work environments that value people, which are fulfilling, it's our responsibility to HELP management to identify the value and return we bring to the table. Building multi-generational teams that want to help one another succeed produces a positive winning environment. There are plenty of stats to back that up, and this book is full of practical "how to's."

The wording is conversational, "big picture," and purpose-driven. The book takes the time to paint a picture for Millennials and Gen Z about how old work environments used to be, and it gives the context of each generation's tendencies and their "why." It uses short comparisons of crucial differences that provide meaning to readers who are new to leadership and who might not even know that generations think differently. The section on professional advancement and the human resources lingo used when hiring leaders and managers is a HUGE value. The advice will help you earn respect in the interview process and with seasoned peers. This book matters. It matters to help win the respect of people from other generations, and prove we don't suck, because our generation is awesome and great!

Brent

Preface

I love working with Millennials and Gen Z. Maybe that's because my children are a part of the Millennial and Gen Z generations. I love them deeply and don't want them to have to enter a workforce led by Gen Xers and Baby Boomers who don't get the flow of our modern society. You may be asking yourself, "Why should you care about what others think, and why should others care about the way you do things?" Millennials and Gen Z want to be "real."

The struggle is real; the first step in making a positive difference in this world, and your life, is to become a leader. All leaders must have followers for nothing great happens without a team. Becoming a great leader that can grow an organization or lead a movement requires a leader that can develop and lead other leaders. "Great" doesn't come just because a person has years of experience. It takes training and applying the art and science of leadership to experience. Open your mind to knowledge and understand that you don't know what you don't know.

Introduction

Welcome!

Thanks for joining with me in learning the art and science of effective leadership. Whether you are a Millennial, Gen Z, Gen X, Baby Boomer, or Traditionalist, you're reading this because of a desire to lead well. Organizations need competent positive leaders! America and the world need you!

Generation Age Group Definitions

There has been much debate on when each generation's birth years begin and end. Pew research is one of the most trusted research sites, so I am using their definitions.

- Traditionalist: Born 1928-1945.
- Baby Boomers: Born 1946-1964.
- Gen X: Born 1965 – 1980.
- Millennials: Born 1981-1996.
- Gen Z: Born 1997 – 2012.[1]

A Note to Gen Z and Millennials

If you're a Millennial or in Gen Z, this book shows you how to win the confidence of Gen Xers and Baby Boomers. You will learn how to prove you don't suck and how to succeed as a leader in a workplace dominated by Gen X and Baby Boomers.

---

[1] (Dimock, 2019)

A Note to Gen X and Baby Boomers

If you're a Gen Xer, this book will help you flourish in a multi-generational workforce and prepare to take the reins as Boomers begin retiring in large numbers. If you're a Boomer, this book provides useful advice on how to mitigate the risk of business interruptions due to the retirement tsunami that is coming, as well as recoup some of the over $550 billion disengaged employees are estimated to cost American corporations.[2]

While this book intends to transfer knowledge to help you become a better leader, its wording has a less formal feel. It's more of a conversation, a book of real-life stories from various business people and places, and it's big-picture and purpose-driven. As you read each story, think about each generation's life experiences, where they are coming from, and why?

A key to unlocking relationships is understanding the other person's "why." Why do they think, act, and react the way they do? When you know, you'll be better positioned to motivate others to follow you no matter what their age.

My greatest wish for the Millennial and Gen Z generations is that they learn how to lead our society and economy to new heights, without all the hang-ups of past generational transitions. Remember, every generation "sucked" to the ones that came before them. As long as we're all in the same boat, let's grow together and improve our workplaces and lives.

---

[2] (Gallup, 2017)

What is Etymology and Why Should I Care?

In the 1970s, when I was in elementary school, we had a teacher who would punish us for using the phrase 'aw shucks.' He told us it was a curse word. WTH, a curse word? Sure enough, at one time, it meant 'oh sh*t' and was considered profanity! Now it is a term that expresses shy embarrassment. [3] The Stack Exchange is a great place to read about a word's past, mainstream, and modern meaning or etymology. Etymology is the study of word origins. As society changes, the essence of words can change or take on more than one meaning. Their use and acceptance may diversify as well.[4] Not only can word meanings change, but each generation adds new words. For example, if you search for terms such as; adulting, woke, salty, kiki, no cap, etc., you can find lots of articles on Millennial and Gen Z lingo.[5] Communication is a two-sided process; make sure to participate effectively.[6] **Ask yourself, "do I practice active listening when talking with members of different generations?"**

In the back of our minds, we know that words and word meanings change over time. Traditionalists, Boomers, and Gen Xers consider the words you got in trouble for saying when you were young. How many of those words, like 'aw-shucks' mean something different now? Never has the essence or meaning behind words changed so quickly as it does today. The digital and Internet age has unleashed society's ability to form new lingo, propagate slang, and modify word meaning. Try reading a Gen Z's text string,

---

[3] (Stack Exchange, n.d.)
[4] (Online Etymology Dictionary, 2019)
[5] (Borge, 2019)
[6] (Pearce, 2007)

good luck if you are over 40! On the flip side, some changes add richness to our life and business experiences. **Either way, we must all realize that what we hear may not be what another person is saying.** If you don't understand something, don't judge, ask for clarification, and practice active listening.

Chapter 1: Getting Your "Why" On

A Dead Leader Walking

In 2017, while in the Caribbean, I met a young American leader who was 28 years old. He had cultivated a following of 15,000 Millennials and paid for his trip by leasing his list of followers to marketing departments. His primary clients were liquor distributors who paid him $5000 every few months to throw flash parties and another $5000-$15,000 to show them how to market their products to Millennials better.

He did a magnificent job of promoting himself through social media, and his parties were epic. The liquor distributors rented the venues, hired bands, set up tasting tables and beer stands, food trucks, etc. His average gathering drew 2000-3000 people. As we talked, I shared some of my corporate leadership experiences, and he asked me some questions. He wanted my opinion on why he hadn't been able to keep a corporate job or obtain promotions. "Why do I keep getting fired," he asked. **"Why don't leaders at work listen to me, I get so frustrated with them, I end up just quitting. Now no one trusts me enough to hire me into a position with responsibility."**

I asked him to explain each situation, and the bottom line was he had no idea how corporations promote people, how HR operates, and that there are measures of employee value. Nor did he respect or relate to other generations. This talented young man thought that he was already a leader because he was able to gather a following on social media. He was right to a degree; he had followers, but for how long?

He understood how to lead a group of young, energetic, party-going peers, and he was great at it, but he had no idea how to be a leader of leaders, produce leaders, or be a leader in any other context. Because he refused to embrace the fact that 50% of leadership is a natural ability, and 50% is a learned science, he never progressed past his current state. He chose not to learn how to expand his reach or sustain his success. **He became a dead leader walking.**

Leadership and Organizational Growth

Here was a talented, smart young person, who could talk to his peers, but had no idea how to interact with or lead his parents' or grandparents' generations. He was bitter because life was more complicated than what his mother had taught him. His mom was always saying, "do the right thing, get good grades, pay attention in school, and you'll get a good job and life will be good." **However, in today's competitive world and economy, doing the basics right doesn't guarantee life will work out the right way.** You must gain specific knowledge and skills to succeed.

He didn't know or understand the five pillars of organization leadership for growth or what it takes to be successful at each one:

- Challenging the status quo with positive innovation.
- Inspiring a vision and set of goals that result in mutual commitment from all employees.
- Building teams that are empowered and are interdependent upon one another to succeed.
- Modeling the behaviors you espouse to others.

- Encouraging the hearts of employees so that they work through difficult times, striving to achieve the mutual vision and goals set before them.[7]

All five pillars of organization leadership for growth require an understanding of how and why each generation thinks the way they do. Gaining an understanding of the assumptions, beliefs, and norms of those you are trying to lead is critical in motivating today's multi-generational, multi-cultural workforce.

How things work out is up to you. There is no magic wand; it takes smarts, hard work, time, education, and wisdom. The dead leader walking's career was severely limited because he didn't know what he didn't know. Don't make the same mistake; choose to learn to lead.

Millennials Don't Suck; They're Awesome

It seems that all I hear from my Gen X and Baby Boomer friends is how Millennials suck. They suck in their work ethic, feel entitled, their attitudes suck, and they don't respect us. "They suck, they suck, they suck." Do you hear the same?

There is a misconception that Millennials are oversensitive, lazy, and uncommitted. Instead, data shows they are passionate, hard workers, and active in social causes. Sessa, Kabacoff, Deal, and Brown's study set out to separate the myths from reality and how the generational differences affect the workplace. Millennials make learning a priority and find happiness in their families.[8] While Millennials may

---

[7] (Johnson & Johnson, 2013)

[8] (Sessa, Kabacoff, Deal, & Brown, 2007)

not be as independent as Gen Xers, they are full of confidence and sensitivity.[9]   Another study done by social scientists, Leuenberger and Klüver, also found that the younger generations desire more frequent feedback than what is provided in annual evaluations.[10]   They want feedback so they can improve their performance. In our diverse workforce, values will differ among the generations based on "beliefs, values, goals, work attitudes, world views, and attitudes toward leadership," which develop throughout our lifetimes.[11]   These values shape our attitudes and willingness to adapt to change.

Emerging leaders, take note! If you, as an emerging leader, bring positive and definite answers to workplace challenges, you will have the chance to establish yourself as a prospective leader and begin building positive relationships with those who can promote you.

Every Generation's Characteristics are Different

Every generation has its own set of characteristics. Gen Z thinks one way, younger Millennials another, older Millennials still another, Gen Xers another, and Baby Boomers, yes...still another. It seems a million books are advising Gen Xers and Baby Boomers on how to lead Millennials, but few, if any, focus on helping Millennials and Gen Z understand how to become leaders.

The analog world in which Boomers and Traditionalists learned to lead, no longer exists. It's time for the Millennial generation to step into leadership roles and lead our

---

[9] (Kapoor & Solomon, 2011)

[10] (Green & Roberts, 2012)

[11] (Sessa, Kabacoff, Deal, & Brown, 2007)

corporations, tech industries, and organizations. It's time for Gen Z to become emergent leaders and start thinking about how they want the world to look over the next century.

We, as senior leaders, need to make way for them, mentor them, and help them understand how we tick, not the other way around. According to Pew Research, there are 56 million Millennials in the workforce, and by 2020 nearly half of all workers will be Millennials, outnumbering Gen Xers![12]

Millennials and Gen Z listen up! The older generations don't have the same world view as you, and if they do, they rank their values in a different priority order than you!
Unless you begin to understand how Gen Xers and Boomers think, you're screwed when it comes to leading us!

Generational Transitions

I was born in 1965 in the first year of Generation X. I grew up in the middle of the transition from an analog to a digital world, from a manufacturing-based economy to a tech and services-based economy. I was an original gamer and Donkey Kong master. I started on Pong, Mattel's classic handheld football games, then Nintendo's RBI Baseball, Zelda, NHL Hockey, and Sega's Sonic the Hedgehog. I gamed my way through every system. Even after I was married and had children, our family's first game console was mine. It was an original Play Station and was a Christmas gift from my wife, (I bought it for myself, wrapped it and labeled it from Mrs. Claus to Santa, LOL)! My favorite game was a flight simulator and Crash Bandicoot. My kids introduced me to Sim City, Medal of Honor, Halo, and others when we got our first Xbox.

---

[12] (Fry, 2018) (Sessa, Kabacoff, Deal, & Brown, 2007)

I'm sure lots of Millennial gamers are reminiscing about their youth right now, and Baby Boomers are wondering what in the world is he saying? That's my point exactly! Although my children grew up as gamers, I don't see the world as Millennials, or Gen Z do, and they don't view the world as I do! Now add Boomers and Traditionalists into the mix, who grew up in an analog world with no digital gaming at all, and that alone is enough to demonstrate how our world views can differ. These world view differences cause communication, relationship, and trust issues!

Let's look backward from a Gen Xer's perspective. I was a first-generation gamer, but a second-generation nerd! My father, a Traditionalist, worked his way up from being an original punch card mainframe coder, to a leader at McDonnell Douglas and IBM's information systems business. He's a first-generation nerd. He used punch cards to code computers. YES, just like in the movie Hidden Figures, he was one of those white shirt, blue tie mainframe computer geeks, and he loved it. He went on to code in FORTRAN and COBOL and then to write much of IBM's original quality assurance and risk management strategies. Even today, he tells me he sometimes dreams in COBOL and writes programs in his sleep! He was a great leader inside and outside of work. However, guess who struggled to connect with his elders and with his children?! That's right, even with all the things we shared, we still had difficulty communicating, having a relationship, and building trust as father and son. Thank God, as we've gotten more mature, we have developed a great relationship.

Every generation seems to say the same thing about the generations that precede and follow them, "We just don't get the _____ generation!" Even though my family had the benefit of being early adopters of technology (my father and I were nerds, and my children and I are gamers), we each have distinct ways in which we see the world. We base what we believe and see upon the society and time in which we each grew up. All generations have differences between them, and generational interactions get even more complicated when considering geographic and regional differences as well. People in California think differently than do Floridians, than do New Yorkers, Texans, Midwesterners, and so on.

Communication, Relationship, and Trust

Each generation's viewpoints have value; understanding them is essential to the growth of the others. We must learn to lead each other. It is vital to facilitate effective communication and have innovative thinking in managing human resources. These elements will help create a work-life balance that will include professional development and well-being while increasing your productivity. Leadership development helps to accomplish these goals.

Thierry Pauchant, Ph.D., professor at Montreal HEC, pointed out that leadership has focused on leaders and their followers rather than the development of leadership.[13] **To gain credibility, a leader must be real, relevant, and respectful of each generation's cultural needs.** For instance, Millennials are not as forgiving as other generations for ineptitude and lack of leadership skills.[14] In other words, Millennials judge leaders more harshly than the older generations do. They forgive of their peers more than their

---

[13] (Green & Roberts, 2012)
[14] (Kapoor & Solomon, 2011)

leaders. These traits make it more challenging for them to develop strong relationships with leaders their age, much less those of older generations. It takes clear, concise, and frequent communication, healthy relationships, and trust to gain followers. **No one is a leader unless they have followers.**

Note to Millennials and Gen Z: If you can't relate and be more tolerant and forgiving of leaders of all ages, you'll stunt your career growth and get passed over for leadership roles. One reason why studying different leadership methods is so important is to overcome this obstacle.

If you struggle with interpersonal relationships, that's ok. You can change that. Coming from a technology background, I know many managers who struggle with interpersonal relationships and social skills. They've often become experts in their field because they were inquisitive. However, when a person is at the expert stage of leadership development they are self-focused. When a person's center of locus is inward (self-centered); they are open to developing neurosis and obsessions. However, if they can learn to shift their center of locus to be external (focused outwardly) on meeting their team members' and superiors' needs, it opens them to see beyond themselves and to build relationships. When a leader's center of locus is external, they can move to the achiever level of leadership. For anyone who wants to build high-performing teams, reaching across generational and cultural lines is critical, and that requires your focus to be on team members, and not yourself. If you are in the expert stage of your career, use your natural curiosity and concentrate on finding out about other person. If you take this approach, people are far more likely to open up to you. Along the way, you will more than likely find common ground upon which to build.

Why Keep Reading this Book?

If you're a Millennial or in Gen Z, and you want to lead, especially if you're going to lead Gen X and Boomers, you're going to have to embrace the struggle and learn how to communicate with the older generations. Understanding why they learned to lead in specific ways and how they view leadership roles is critical. It's time to start building trusted relationships with other generations.

If you're a Gen Xer or Boomer, and you want to raise the next generation of leaders and grow your business, "deal with it," the world has changed. Our economy is no longer based on manufacturing. Leadership styles, like command and control, are no longer respected or effective. Machiavellian principled leadership styles are offensive to today's workers, and qualified talent will not stay if led that way. We must learn how to communicate, have relationships, and build strong trust bonds with our children's generation. It's our responsibility to lead by example and bring positive change, bettering everyone's work-life balance while maintaining workplace effectiveness.

Reflections

Take five minutes and reflect on what you've learned. Write down at least three takeaways. At the end of the book you will have 30+ key ideas to review that will help mold your thinking, build bridges, and bolster your leadership skills.

1._____

_____

_____

_____

_____

2._____

_____

_____

_____

_____

3._____

_____

_____

_____

_____

_____

_____

_____

_____

Chapter 2: Leaders Are Dropping Like Flies

A Tsunami is Forming

On August 13, 1868, in New Zealand, business leaders and workers were going about their daily routines, mothers were preparing their children for school, and planning the day's activities and chores. No one expected that shortly their lives and the lives of their countrymen would be changed forever. Thousands of miles away, one of the most massive earthquakes in modern history struck South America. It was approximately 9.0 on the Richter scale. The quake's shock wave started a wave in the Pacific Ocean. As it traveled across the ocean, the swell grew larger and larger, forming a massive tsunami. Hours later, without warning, 25,000 souls passed into the afterlife, hundreds of businesses were devastated, and damages totaled $300 million.[15]

When unprepared, tsunamis can be a devastating event. This same type of event repeated itself over and over until modern-age communication and meteorological technology began to predict and warn people of these events. Even so, on March 11, 2011. Thirty-three-foot waves traveling 500 miles per hour struck a nuclear power plant in Japan, creating one of the most significant nuclear disasters of our lifetime. At that time, the World Bank estimated that it would take five years to recover from the $235 billion in financial devastation and the 452,000 displaced people resulting from the tsunami.[16] The results were stress on the global supply chain for more than two years.

---

[15] (eCoast, 2018)
[16] (Phillips, 2011)

The generational shift in the workforce is swelling. **The U.S. Department of Labor predicts a significant shift in the makeup of the workforce.**[17] The resulting tsunami of change will open leadership doors for Millennial and Gen Z employees to advance into leadership faster than earlier generations. The question is, will they (you) be ready to fill the tens of thousands of vacant leadership roles that are coming? If we, as current leaders, do not help support this transition, what will happen? What will be the cost?

Current leaders, we must prepare and grow emergent leaders by learning to communicate with and value each other and our differences. Emerging leaders need to engage in leadership training. If we do our parts, we'll help ensure smooth leadership transitions and avoid business disruptions due to lackluster leadership benches.

We Need a New Wave of Leaders

As our nation's workforce ages at an alarming rate, the warning signals are telling us to prepare, but will we do so? If we are to weather the coming generational shift and retirement storm, we must begin to create new leaders from the younger generations, pass on our leadership wisdom, and prepare the way for them. To accomplish this task, corporate leaders will need to understand and sponsor:

- Millennial and Gen Z team work ethics.
- Mentor and reverse mentor emerging leaders.
- Re-invigorate disengaged employees.
- Attract and retain top talent.

---

[17] (U.S. Bureau of Labor Statistics, 2019)

- How to modernize and expand communication channels.
- Win the hearts of emerging leaders through sustainable leadership.
- Incorporate transformational and servant-based leadership ideals.
- Identify potential leaders.
- Manage a kaleidoscope of assumptions, beliefs, and norms.
- Build trust and relationships with multiple generations.
- Re-evaluate their team's generational diversity.

The U.S. Department of Labor reports that younger generations are entering the workforce later, and portions of the older generations are working longer. Those who are working later in life are filling jobs normally filled by 16 to 24-year-old workers. The younger generations are taking longer to graduate from college and therefore enter the workforce later. **Teams are becoming more diverse in their generational makeup.** Leaders will have to know how to relate, motivate, and lead people from all generations. The Department of Labor predicts this trend to continue until 2028.[18]

We must take this opportunity to ready ourselves and our businesses to avoid the devastating effects of having a shallow pool of leaders. No one should expect new and emerging leaders to navigate the coming turbulent waters unless we train and support them.

---

[18] (U.S. Bureau of Labor Statistics, 2019)

Catch the Vibe, Ride the Wave

In 2001, I was living in Atlanta, but working for our Scottsdale, AZ, division. Every other week I flew into Scottsdale and then back home to manage the Atlanta facility. For the past year, there had been changes happening in the human resources and marketing divisions, and the company hired a new senior vice president of marketing (SVP). The first project she gave our team was to start documenting our knowledge. Writing down our learned knowledge threw up red flags for me. Once we wrote down our intellectual property (IP), stored it on our hard drives, and uploaded it into the shared enterprise content management (ECM) system, the vast majority of us would no longer be needed. (BTW - at the time, the storage technology was cutting edge, using "the cloud," impressive, huh?!). I tried to warn my colleagues that a reduction in force (RIF) was coming, but they laughed me off. They thought, "after all, the company still needs people, right?"

While they sat comfortably at their desks, working on the documentation project, I reached out to another company in our industry. One that we beat all the time using the marketing and sales strategies I had created. I figured they would jump at the chance to hire the person who was authoring the approach to which they were losing, and I was right. They thought I would bring a lot of value to their team and could help them turn their sales revenue around, and I did!

As we negotiated my employment package, I continued to give 110% to my current employer and finished the documentation project. A few weeks later, I flew into Scottsdale, AZ, as usual, only to walk into a building with the oddest, somber atmosphere I had ever experienced.

Several people in grey suits greeted me, and there were two armed guards in each hallway. The "suits" asked me to follow them quietly, and they took me to one of our meeting rooms where my colleagues were sitting. I thought to myself, "This is so bizarre!" I asked one of my friends what was going on, and he let me know that the new SVP had flown in with her HR team and was handing out severance packages! I had walked into a corporate wake and was attending the division's funeral. Even the air inside the building felt heavy and sad!

This atmosphere was completely different than it had been the past few years. Usually, this was the happiest and most fun-filled work environment in which I had ever worked. We were known for being the creative innovation hub for the entire $3 billion, 30,000 employee operation. We had the freedom to build a creative, innovative atmosphere. We were the first to adopt business casual attire, and on Fridays the guys could wear jeans, and the women sundresses, and who cared if we wore open-toed shoes that day?! Heck, half of us wore Nikes and sandals. What's even more remarkable, is that our offices were across the street from the PGA TPC course, and we would grab hotdogs and hit a bucket of balls for lunch at the driving range (drop mic)!

Note to Millennials and Gen Z: To understand how creative and progressive our division was, let's contrast it to the rest of the company. If you were in sales, the managers required suit and ties for the men, and suit or dress for the woman, with no open-toed shoes. The office layout placed managers' offices along the walls, while everyone else sat at five-foot-wide cubical style desks. Your desk had a tower computer (PC) that sat under your desk and a landline phone. Each person had to report in at 8:00 am, tell their manager which customers they were going to visit that day, come back to the office no later than 4:30 pm and report on the day's events. Even if you lived in your sales territory, you still had to make these useless drives! You would have to drive out of your area to report to the office and then drive back, even if it was an hour each way! What a waste of time (BTW mind blown yet? If not, keep reading.).

Asking to telecommute (work remote) meant you were lazy, you couldn't be trusted, there must be something wrong with you, or you were most likely interviewing with another company, and they should probably fire you. Many sales compensation plans used a recoverable draw commission system. If you don't know what that is, ask an old-timer. It meant, if you didn't sell anything or meet your quota, you had to pay back your salary. That's why it's called a draw. The company gave you an advance or a "draw" against your monthly sales. If you didn't sell, you owed them!

Let's get back to the story. The issue was, depending on which senior leader you asked, we were either innovative leaders or complete corporate rebels! To the gloom-and-doom "starched-shirt ice queen of the Northeast" new SVP, we were rebels. She didn't like our style, and she was there to shut us down. One by one, I watched my friends get RIFed. Three, six, and nine-month severance packages were handed out, depending on the length of employment. If you were lucky enough to receive a job offer, the entire operation was moving to the Northeast.

While I was observing the ominous events, my director walked in and asked why I was in the room. We went to his office, and he explained that the new SVP was firing 75 out of 110 of our staff members. Not because they sucked, we were the second most innovative industry program in the nation, but because the new SVP was a Traditionalist. She saw our creative culture as a threat to the way she thought. She was a laggard and hated our creative atmosphere. She liked to have command and wanted to squeeze everyone to fit inside her little traditional box. Although my director, my teammates, and I had kept our positions and gained more clout, I had already packed my parachute. I jumped to a smaller $1 billion company with better upward mobility. Moreover, I landed higher in leadership and took my first national role.

What's the moral of this story? Business seasons have signs. Like surfing in the ocean, if you pay attention, you can predict when a wave is coming, feel its vibe, and ride it to a better place. **Are you aware of the business environment surrounding you?** Don't be like my former peers and get swallowed up in the wash.

Waves of Change

During that season of my career, I experienced a rogue wave. Rogue waves are those that are in the middle of the ocean, stick up higher than the others, but don't affect the direction of the primary current. We had made transformative headway into a more modern way of doing business. We were riding a real wave; we were innovative leaders. However, a rogue wave, in the form of a laggard SVP from another era, with outdated ideas, fighting against the flow of change came in and shut us down. Her only legacy was one of domination and destruction.

From that time on, the company struggled to grow. The board of directors made more poor appointments and hired a lackluster CEO, its stock lost 50% of its value, and people lost hundreds of thousands of dollars from their retirement accounts. Another traditionally managed company eventually acquired the company, and in 2018 it had to restructure, cutting 4000 jobs, and it is at risk of bankruptcy. Today, Glassdoor.com rates it as a "Stay Away." **Watch out for rogue waves and be aware of real current changes in the primary flow.**

Business seasons and work environments have an atmosphere, a temperature, a feeling, a vibe, and analytical markers that point out the primary flow's direction. If we are actively listening, we'll recognize that we talk about these change indicators in our social conversations, over dinner, drinks, or a glass of wine. One evening my wife and I, who are Gen Xers, were at our friends' house for dinner. Six of our close friends (three couples) joined us. Two of the couples are Baby Boomers, and two are Gen Xers like us. When we arrived, we hugged and gave welcome kisses (on the cheek, LOL) as usual. After a short time chatting, the gals went into the dining room, and the guys sat in the living room. As the guys updated each other on life, they asked me about my doctoral studies and the subject of this book.

Note: The names have been changed to protect the innocent, LOL!

Chuck began talking about how fascinated he was with my research on workplace behavior on leadership and the generations. He joked about how he likes to watch funny videos about Millennials on the web. Chuck works for the government and said they have generation diversity classes on how to work with other generations. He started discussing common perceptions of Millennials from his Baby Boomer perspective. As soon as he began, Jim, a Baby

Boomer, and John, a Gen Xer, started chiming right in. They were each telling stories about how Millennials had helicopter parenting, participation trophies, lack of work ethic, feelings of entitlement, and no sense of commitment to anything. *Millennials need to adjust to the way they see the world, just like we were expected to by our leaders.* Then turning to me, they asked if my in-depth look showed the same things. **Are Millennials really like that?**

Most Boomers and Gen X leaders are interested in working with and understanding the younger generations. Chuck attended all the generational diversity training classes he could. He also asked me lots of questions over the next six months. I was able to share a different point of view about Millennials and Gen Z than portrayed in the media. I hope I helped him in some small way because he is now running an entire government division. Crossing the generational "aisle" pays off. Consider reaching out and striking up a conversation with other generations. **Realize the other generations are just as uncomfortable facing the wave of change as you,** and Gen Xers feel trapped by the generational shift.

Gen X: A Wave of Dissatisfaction

The undertow of workplace dissatisfaction is pulling Gen X down. They've already been hit by a change wave, and their needs are being overlooked at work. They are called the forgotten generation, and that's how they feel. They are more likely to be passed over for promotions more often than their younger and older counterparts.[19] They are the most unhappy work generation since the founding of

---

[19] (Craver, 2019)

America.[20] There are many reasons for this. For instance, the fear of being replaced, losing their job, and the consequences that may follow, i.e., not being able to support their families. Operational strategists realize a typical Gen Xer will put in long stress-filled work hours, without complaining or jumping from job to job. They use these fears against them when it comes to workplace concessions and the environment in which they work.[21] Gen Xers watch their needs go unmet, while the company makes changes to accommodate Millennial needs.

Gen Xers are rethinking their quality of life. It is becoming more frequent for mid-career Gen Xers to leave their lucrative roles to find work that is more fulfilling and enjoyable. They are picking up on the trend of work-life balance.[22]

The Great Wave of Disengaged Workers

Gen X's disenchantment with work, and Traditionalists' and Boomers' impending retirements are fueling workforce disengagement. In the private business sector, only 33% of American employees are engaged at work as compared to the world's best organizations where 70% of workers are engaged.[23] The cost of disengaged employees for U. S. companies is $483 billion to $605 billion a year, yet **leaders and managers who focus on employees' strengths can eliminate workforce disengagement**.[24]

---

[20] (Hill, 2019)

[21] (Eisenberg, 2019)

[22] (Hill, 2019)

[23] (Sorenson & Garman, 2013)

[24] (Gallup, 2017)

Chances are you have at least one disengaged worker in your office. They're the ones who are there but aren't there. The ones who never have an answer, and always expect the workgroup to make up for the work they don't get done. Dreaming of retirement is just one reason why employees become disengaged. Other causes are; burnout, disenchantment with current managers, the lack of mentoring, and limited upward mobility. At some point in their careers, many people experience at least one of these.

Note to Emerging Leaders: Providing answers that recoup some of the lost revenue spent on disengaged workers is a terrific way to prove your worth as a leader. One modern strategy to do so is called Appreciative Inquiry (AI). It is a set of skills based on positive psychology. Current and emerging leaders should develop these skills, and we will talk more about them in later chapters. These skills help combat disengagement from the beginning and help disengaged workers re-engage. AI focuses on employee and company strengths. It is a positive, healthy leadership strategy. Leaders also need to recognize equality and diversity in the workplace and use them as positive sources of energy and not division.[25] An excellent strategy to be recognized as a leader at work is to use AI techniques, such as engaging in "World Café" style meetings.[26]

The Monster Wave of Retiring Leaders

In the **United States government sector, almost 60% of employees are eligible to retire**, and the "senior management cohort consists mainly of Baby Boomers, which is setting the stage for conflict with the post-

---

[25] (Sorenson & Garman, 2013)
[26] (The World Cafe', 2019)

modernism orientation of the Generation X and Millennials that are replacing retiring employees."[27] Research also identified that the government is concerned that **their human capital is at "high risk"** and that unless management takes this issue seriously, **they will be looking at a "retirement tsunami."**[28] There's a monster wave of change swelling in the workplace's makeup as Traditionalists disappear, Boomers prepare to retire, and the number of Millennials who are entering the workplace increases.[29]

This monster wave has been swelling for a while, and it's getting ready to crest. If you're going to successfully navigate and ride this monster, and take your place in leadership, you're going to need to be a(n):

- Overcomer.
- Sincere communicator.
- Relationship builder.
- Emotionally and culturally woke.
- Creative innovator.
- Team builder.
- Bridge-building, chasm-crossing, gap-filling, motivational leader.

To ride this wave, current and emerging leaders need to work together. This merging of the generations needs a coordinated effort to make sure that upper management transfers its experiential wisdom and organizational knowledge to its emerging leaders. We must bridge the

---

[27] (Green & Roberts, 2012)
[28] (Green & Roberts, 2012)
[29] (Fry, 2018)

gaps between Traditionalists, Baby Boomers, Generation X, Millennials, and Gen Z.[30]

Today's business climate, its indicators, its temperature, its vibe, is one pointing to a wave of millions of people who are re-evaluating their lives, disengaged at work, and focused on retiring. There is a wave swelling for the need for tens of thousands of new leaders. Prepare yourself and get trained. Position yourself to fill a more vital role and to have more responsibility, and increased pay. **You want to ride this wave!**

---

[30] (Green & Roberts, 2012)

Reflections

Take five minutes and reflect on what you've learned. Write down at least three takeaways. At the end of the book you will have 30+ key ideas to review that will help mold your thinking, build bridges, and bolster your leadership skills.

1._____

_____

_____

_____

_____

_____

2._____

_____

_____

_____

_____

_____

3._____

_____

_____

_____

_____

_____

_____

_____

_____

_____

Chapter 3: Differences in Value Systems

The Priority Difference in Values

In one of my entrepreneurial ventures, I developed a "three-legged stool" business plan for myself and two close friends. All three of us were from different generations and had the same values. The business plan would only work if each of us executed our part as written. Each of us was an expert in our respective areas, and the venture was a smashing success at first, but as time progressed, a fracture opened and became very apparent to two of us. The third person was utterly blind to the issue. The problem was, although we valued the same things, we ranked them differently.

For the younger two of us, family, friendship, loyalty, and integrity come before money and business. The older of us valued his legacy and finances first, then family, loyalty, and integrity. In the end, when it came time for the third person to contribute to the business, he saw how critical his input was, and he refused to work unless we provided additional remuneration in advance, which was beyond our original agreement. In essence, he held us hostage. You can imagine the pain we felt! Here was someone we had known for years holding our families hostage over money!

After we parted ways, I sought advice on how to avoid this situation in the future. Another friend pointed out that the third person was a Traditionalist, based on his life experiences; his values were not in the same priority as a Gen Xer or Millennial. To the Traditionalist, he was "doing" business; to the rest of us, he was betraying our trust and hurting our families. To this day, the gentleman has no idea how much his actions hurt us, how damaging they were to the venture, or how wrong they were to our generations.

Why did the older of us put money and business before our friendship? He was a Traditionalist. He had gone through the depression, WWII, and knew what it was like to see soup lines and be homeless. His life experiences imprinted his mind to value money and business as his top priorities. Traditionalists and Boomers have the need and importance of material goods high on their list of priorities. Why? It is a product of the society in which they grew up.

The Value of Finding Acceptance in Workgroups

It's a typical day in the office, and an 11:00 am Monday morning team meeting has just started. The department's director Sue, who is a long-term employee and Gen Xer, is facilitating the meeting. Attending are four first-level managers: Bob, a Boomer; Bill, a Gen Xer; Arden, a Millennial who just got promoted into management; and Amber, a Millennial who is two years into her management position; and their teams. Sue wants ideas for new strategies on how to best approach several interoffice operational issues. During the meeting, Arden and his team dominate the conversations. The meeting ends at noon, and Bob and Bill, grab lunch in the building's cafeteria, they buy today's special and sit down. Bob starts the conversation...

"Bill, what was that?! These damn Millennials are so arrogant it's unbelievable, can you believe that Arden just let his team run off at the mouth. Does he think he can come in here and take over, tell us what to do like we've been idiots all these years?" Bill responds, "Bob, I hear you. He's the FNG and came in spouting out ideas like he's a tenured member of the team! Who does he think he is? His momma probably pampered and rescued him from failing too. They think they're entitled to everything. What kind of name is Arden anyway?!" Bob says, "Classic CLM! He's gotta learn around here; it's ETR baby, ETR!"

Note to Millennials and Gen Z: ETR (Earn the right), FNG (F'n New Guy/Girl), and CLM (Career Limiting Move).

At the same time, Arden and Amber walk a half block down from the office to a great coffee and tea café' where they have shared workspaces. Arden is having a cup of kava and Amber, a shaken black tea, iced with three pumps. Arden starts the conversation...

"I felt Bob personally attacked me in our meeting today. My team and I tried our best to offer up ideas, and all he did was make us feel like our ideas sucked. I'm not sure if I want to continue being a manager here. Maybe I should go where I'm appreciated." Amber responds, "I hear you, Arden, I felt the same way when I got promoted. Every time I tried to give input, Sue always cut me off, like I was some plebe. I felt like the woman in the commercial who's presenting to a workgroup of monkeys." Arden, "I bet they couldn't even download the presentation to their iPhones...idiots. I can't wait until they retire; of course, I'll probably be long gone by then." Amber laughs and then retorts, "Actually Sue and I talked, I told her how I felt, and she was shocked. She didn't mean to make me feel rejected or unappreciated. I think we get each other now."

A Note to Xers, Boomers and Traditionalists: Kava (nature's Xanax) is a drink that looks muddy and relaxes you without dulling mental sharpness. A shared workspace is a place from which people can work outside the office and can help release innovative, creative flow.

One of the areas affecting team building is when and how new team members find acceptance and a voice within workgroups; this is called team membership negotiation. No matter the generation, this process takes place over time. However, Millennials, in general, have grown up with a sense of self-worth and acceptance due to hovering or helicoptering parenting techniques, which focus on self-esteem, coaching without allowing consequences, and the belief that everyone has value. These ideas and parenting styles are different than those of older generations. Some of these aspects were good, but the application of them was not. One failure was that self-esteem is different from self-respect. Psychologists have found that it is self-respect that builds strong interpersonal skills.[31] Having been raised with an emphasis on self-esteem has caused Millennials to believe they have automatic acceptance within a group. However, their elder peers require a person to ETR. As time progresses, this assumed acceptance can cause friction with older members and stifle the acceptance process.[32]

Research shows that there are differences in perceived work ethic, as well. These differences may create additional barriers to being accepted within new workgroups. As different work norm beliefs surface, disparities in accepted practices may make older group members marginalize younger newcomers. The marginalization intensifies with lower-level communication skills, which lack understanding of each generation's preferred communication methods.

---

[31] (Langer, 2016)
[32] (Myers & Sadaghiani, 2010)

Gen Xers notoriously dislike group work and meetings, yet Millennials have grown up in workgroup environments and meeting in groups from grade school through university studies.

Group and team environments have a great deal of importance in acceptance in the workplace. Millennials grew up as the center of attention. Mid-career Gen Xers in middle management don't see as much need for group work; they desire to work autonomously.[33] Millennials also want to know detailed knowledge of strategic information, generally reserved for upper managers. They tend to reject the idea that information is provided on a "need to know" basis.[34] This drive to see private or privileged information can cause trust issues with older leaders.

A marked commonality is that the generations are equally concerned about success and money.[35] Regarding a positive impact on workplace performance and team building, Millennials want frequent, open, detailed, and positive support from their managers. Growing up in an environment in which parents, teachers, and coaches sent recurring, positive re-enforcement messages to help Millennials learn, these same children, now adults, expect the same in the workplace. The challenge is that most middle managers, who are typically Gen Xers, do not want to answer their frequent questions or coach them. As a result, middle managers see Millennials as needy, and without the ability to stand on their own two feet. Being aware of these differences will help you choose when to ask for assistance and do it wisely. Leaders love it when people

---

[33] (Myers & Sadaghiani, 2010)
[34] (Myers & Sadaghiani, 2010)
[35] (Hershatter & Epstein, 2010)

show self-initiative, research a problem, and bring positive solutions to the table.

The Value of Mentorship

In 2013, a professor asked a group of university students to collaborate on a project. After completing it, the professor asked them to provide an independent private evaluation of their group peers. Incredibly, all five group members gave each other the same rating in every category!

The professor scolded them, asking why they had given each other the same ratings. The leader responded by telling the professor, "Your instructions were contradictory to everything you've taught us this semester." The professor was shocked, "How dare you tell me my instructions were contradictory; I've been teaching for 30 years. I specifically told each of you to rate your team members independently based upon their performances." The student leader responded, "Exactly! All semester you have graded us as a group, and now you want us to rat each other out, no way."

The professor, shocked at the student's viewpoint, pushed pause and thought for a moment. He then asked, "Do you understand the difference between collusion and collaboration?" They all answered, "Yes, however, this was a collaborative project, and we all share equally in our grade."[36] Technically the students colluded on giving each other the same grade and historically that is unethical.

Although the students expressed that they understood the terminology, they didn't embrace the same legal or ethical

---

[36] (VanMeter, Grisaffe, Chonko, & Roberts, 2013)

viewpoint of collusion as the professor. The students didn't know what they didn't know, or did they?

Many members of the older generations believe in meritocracy, which is the distribution of wealth, resources, and responsibility according to merit (worthy of the reward by earning it), and not need. Those who contribute more valuably to a society, a workgroup, or a college project receive greater rewards. However, the students believed in equal distribution, i.e., they all pitched in, some more than others, but in the end, they were in it as a group. Today there is an ongoing debate on these subjects in our nation. Distributive justice is a hot topic in most nations' economic-political systems.

This story is just one example of how life's experiences and society form each generation's characteristics. There are hundreds of surveys filled with stories like the one above. Hundreds of thousands of Millennials have detailed their generation's attitudes, aspirations, societal, and organizational impressions.[37] Each generation has different perspectives, ways of thinking, accepted social behaviors, communication styles, and belief systems.

Mentoring programs can assist with bridging these differences in viewpoints. There is a need to instill the value of meritocracy in the workforce. There is also a need for positive support systems from managers to subordinates. Mentoring programs can deliver both. These needs stem from the reality that many Millennial employees were raised by parents, teachers, coaches, and others who made them feel accepted regardless of their performance or the outcome

---

[37] (Hershatter & Epstein, 2010)

of their work. The sense of entitlement and auto-acceptance in the Millennial generation is pervasive.[38]

Mentors and mentees must be aware of the differences in communication norms and be prepared to adapt. As children, Millennials were encouraged to speak and interact with adults, teachers, and coaches. The effect has been the propensity to interrupt managers and superiors, causing difficulties in relationships, respect, and middle management's ability to get their work completed. One generation sees interruptions as disrespectful, while the other sees them as their opportunity to provide input. Better expectation setting through mentorship can mitigate difficulties in communication styles.

The great news is that younger generations want and welcome mentorship. They are eager to learn but ask mentors to treat them with equal respect. Mentorship should never make another person feel subpar. The whole idea of mentoring is to pass on the skills and knowledge that comes with experience.

The Value of Hard Work

Millennials and Gen Z, please understand that the older generations learned that hard work is a character trait and that working long hard hours brings self-worth. They typically believe the more successful you are, the higher your income will be, and the more stuff you can buy. Many also believe that owning more stuff creates happiness and raises self-esteem.

---

[38] (Hershatter & Epstein, 2010)

While they were growing up and maturing into adults, American businesses were encouraged by industry marketing consultants like Victor Lebow, to convince the public to adopt materialism as its source of personal ego and spiritual satisfaction.[39] It was part of the corporate marketing strategy put into play in the 1950s. It embraced Darwinism and Aristotle's Nicomachean Ethics. Even President Eisenhower's economic advisors espoused the idea that the main purpose of the government at that time was to promote economic growth. Not to build schools, take care of our nation's citizens, or any other socially responsible activities, but produce economic wealth. The stronger our economic position, the better we could fund our military and protect ourselves against our enemies and the ideas of communism and socialism.

As horrible as that sounds today, America had just been through the Great Depression and WWII, was at war with Korea and was now facing the effects of the Cold War. Schools were performing nuclear bomb safety exercises and being a "doomsday prepper" was considered normal. If you were fortunate enough to have the money, you had a bomb shelter in your back yard right next to the children's swing set! Considering those circumstances, the reasoning for the choices made and the pathways taken by our elected government officials and corporate leaders is more understandable. It doesn't make it right, but understandable.

Boomers and Gen Xers, please understand that our current society teaches our children that there is more to life than hard work. Today's generations see work as a tool that helps build the lifestyle a person wants to live. If a person wants to

---

[39] (Lebow, 1955)

live in a tiny house and travel, then the type of work they choose supports that lifestyle. They believe in work, they just don't live to work.

The Value of Environmental Responsibility

Growing up in a Midwestern industrial city, the sound of freight trains, the smell of factory smoke, the noise of F-15 fighter jets conducting practice flights at McDonnell Douglas' Lambert Airport facility were just part of life. There were countless TV news stories on the local environment. For example, the EPA had to close our soccer fields because there were toxic waste dumps next to them. Dioxin poisoning forced the closing of entire neighborhoods. Across the Mississippi River near the Shell oil refinery, news stations shot video of smoke and fire trailing behind children as they rode their bikes through mercury saturated drainage ditches.

Just recently, in June of 2018, my brother and I found out that radioactive material had been pouring out into our neighborhood creek since the 1960s.[40] We lived near Cold Water Creek from 1979 to 1989. Although our motocross trail was next to it, thank God, and I mean that sincerely, we never got in the water!

Hopefully, my childhood experiences will help provide some insight into the forming of Gen X's views of environmental responsibility and sustainability. We were the generation of kids who first saw TV commercials and ad campaigns to stop littering and to respect our lands. One of the most iconic Public Service Announcements (PSAs) of the 1970s was the "Keep America Beautiful" commercials

---

[40] (Bernhard, 2018)

featuring a native American Indian crying as he watched American corporations poison the land with trash and chemical runoff. Think about that, mindfulness for preserving our natural resources and environment only began one generation ago! To get a deeper understanding of Gen X's life experiences, you can view the PSAs on YouTube by searching for "Keep America Beautiful - 1973".[41]

Turning to organizational growth, traditionally, there are three G's of growth; consistent growth, competitive growth, and profitable growth. In today's business environment, these traditional corporate ideals are not enough to win the minds and hearts of environmentally conscious people. Our corporate cultures must embrace and adopt a fourth G, that is, responsible growth, which creates social wealth. Companies such as Whole Foods are making active headway into Conscious Capitalism,[42] where companies learn to make steady profits while doing good. Learn more at www.consciouscapitalism.org. Organizations can also apply to be a B Corporation, which certifies that their business practices are sustainable and responsible. Search YouTube for "B Corporations" to find out more or go to www.bcorporation.net.[43]

Part of a Gen Xer's life experience is the abuse of the earth and by corporate and government leaders who didn't care. Traditionalists' minds were imprinted by their experiences to be concerned about having enough food to eat and money to pay rent than keeping the environment clean. Boomers were busy getting their spiritual and ego needs met

---

[41] (Public Service Announcement, 1973)

[42] (Conscious Capitalism, 2019)

[43] (BCorporation, 2019)

by obtaining "stuff," and the well-being of the earth and our environment was an afterthought.

Why was this the case? Traditionalists not only suffered through the scarcities of the Great Depression but also the death and sacrifices made during WWII and the Korean War. Until recently, 2005 - 2010, America has not known a time where masses of people were homeless. During those years, high unemployment rates forced mass foreclosures. People had no choice but to live in their cars or tent cities like the Hoovervilles of the 1930s.[44] Even stars like Kelly Clarkson said she was living in her car when she tried out for American Idol. After the wars, many people, fathers and mothers, and brothers and sisters came back with broken bodies and marred memories. No one knew about post-traumatic stress disorder (PTSD), much less offering them treatment. As a result, differing generational characteristics, ideas, attitudes, and coping mechanisms developed from open wounds that never healed.

It will be interesting to see the effects on the members of Gen Z whose parents lost their homes, lived in tent cities, cars, and shelters. What will the effect be on the children who lived their formative years in modern US tent cities.[45] How will their beliefs, values, and norms be affected? In his book, *"The Wealth of Nations"*, the father of capitalism, Adam Smith, said, "If you want to serve your self-interest, you will do what's best for society."[46] A true capitalist keeps his neighbor and customer's best interest in mind. All people should appreciate the social consciousness of the Millennial and Gen Z generations.

---

[44] (Gregory, 2009)
[45] (Associated Press, 2008)
[46] (Smith, 1776)

A Note to Gen Z, Millennials, and Gen X, if you want to understand Traditionalists and their Baby Boomer children, dig into their life experiences. One of the best videos I've seen to help understand the propensity to sacrifice the earth for material goods is *"The Story of Stuff."* Before you continue reading, please take a few minutes and watch the video at www.TheStoryofStuff.org or on YouTube at https://youtu.be/9GorqroigqM.[47]

Note to Gen X, Boomers, and Traditionalists: If you want to understand why Gen Z and Millennials are environmentally and socially conscious, I highly recommend watching "The Story of Stuff" as well. It may also give you insights into your generation.

The Value of Sustainability

During Harish Manwani, former Chairman and COO of Unilever's TED Talk, he stated that capitalism had done a lot of great things, but it has not kept up with all the needs of society. Corporations must help support the communities that support them. The question then becomes, how do we do well in business and do good at the same time. It must come through leadership. Two things that are non-negotiable for leaders are your values and your purpose.[48]

Mr. Manwani joined Unilever, the world's largest soap manufacturer, in 1976. He was appointed to the Board of Directors in 1995, as Director for Personal Products business. In 2000, he moved to the UK as Senior Vice President for the Global Hair Care and Oral Care categories.

---

[47] (Creative Commons License, 2009)
[48] (Manwani, 2013)

In early 2001, Unilever appointed him as President - Home and Personal Care, Latin America Business Group. Since 2005, he assumed charge as the Non-Executive Chairman of the company.[49]

On his first day at work in 1976, his boss directed him that he was there to change live s, not just to manufacture personal care products. Simple acts like children washing their hands save lives. Worldwide, 5-million children die annually because of infections that washing their hands would prevent. This fact prompted Unilever to create and run the largest handwashing social initiative in the world. Unilever also runs programs that help women in developing nations. One such program is Shakti. Shakti is Unilever's program for women, which teaches them how to create and run small nutritional businesses. These businesses spread the word on nutrition and hygiene, which in turn changes lives for the better. In 2018, 97,000 women were in the program. These socially responsible ways of creating wealth are improving and helping India's society to be healthier as well as benefiting the corporation financially.

Unilever is also working on using 100% sustainable raw materials in its food products. For instance, non-sustainably sourced Palm Oil is the cause of 20% of India's deforestation. As Unilever's policies change, so will the deforestation. All these good things are happening because their leadership values human life, and they have purposed to change the lives of consumers while they market soap and soup.

Business leaders need to realize they should not just be about selling products. Unilever is a great example, where its

---

[49] (Unilever PLC, 2005)

mission is not just about selling soap. It is about making sure that their business process changes people's lives. Their small actions are making big differences. Unilever's Sustainable Living Plan states, "Our purpose is to make sustainable living commonplace."[50] To do well while doing good, they produce high-quality detergents that use less water. If all people used reduced water soaps, it would save 500 billion liters of water annually; enough to supply the continent of Asia for one month.

The topic of warring over water rights is a growing international topic on sustainability. It is getting so prevalent that in the 2008 James Bond movie, "*Quantum of Solace*"[51], the plot centered around real events based on a water war that happened in Bolivia. The Bolivian government sold not only the rights to its groundwater but also its rain. The government jailed people for collecting rainwater to drink! Water is not just a foreign or developing nation's issue, ask the actor Tom Selleck. In 2015, the county he lives in sued him for stealing public water.[52]

Note to All: To get more information, go to the Public Broadcasting System's shop website, www.shop.PBS.org, and search for "*Blue Gold: World Water Wars.*"[53]

The Value of a Positive Work-Life Balance

In one of the advanced courses I taught, I was talking with a gentleman who was in his 40s. His company promoted him up a level a year earlier. We were discussing some of the

---

[50] (Unilever, 2019)
[51] (Forster, 2008)
[52] (Associated Press, 2015)
[53] (Bozzo & McDowel, 2008)

ways that his life had changed; he traveled more, had more spending money, was able to take better vacations, etc. Then I asked, "What's a typical workday like?" After he described his workday, I asked, "How do you decompress?" At that moment, he realized that he had started drinking more, not only more frequently, but also in larger quantities. I asked, "Are you drinking more just on the road or at home as well?" He answered, "Both." I asked, "Why?" He said, "This new role is so stressful, if I head straight home without decompressing, I get irritable and end up getting in a fight with my wife or yelling at my children. When my head is still at work, it's hard to talk with my children." I agreed, "It's good to decompress, but what are the consequences of drinking to decompress?" He thoughtfully answered, "Less time with my children, less communication with my wife, less marital intimacy." I then asked, "How much of your raise is going toward stress relief?" At that point, he started to realize his promotion at work was a demotion in quality of life. Stress was eating the benefits of his raise, and he was choosing unhealthy ways to deal with it. The promotion tipped his work-life balance in the wrong direction. Let's get real, to truly wake him up; I had to ask, "How much is the divorce and family counseling going to cost?"

A different way of looking at taking a promotion or making a career change is when I took my first 50% travel role. I got together with my wife, and we took the time to measure how many hours I had at home when I was working at the corporate headquarters, versus how many I would have working from a home office and traveling. What we found was that due to rush hour traffic, working late, and when my children had to go to bed (so they could get up for school), I would gain four to eight hours of family time a week. By working from home when I wasn't traveling, I ended up with more family time! For me, my stress level went down, I had more time with my family, and I was making more money - a win-win-win.

The importance of a healthy work-life balance is an area in which other generations can learn from Millennials and Gen Z. That's right I said it, Gen X, Boomers, and Traditionalists can learn some things from Millennials and Gen Z. We can glean some healthy behaviors from them. Millennials and Gen Z work to live; in other words, the money they earn supports the lifestyle of their choice.

Quality of life and a healthy work-life balance were not even a thought for most Traditionalists or Boomers. Many Gen Xers watched our parents' homes torn apart over work, finances, and other stuff, to the point that 50% of all marriages ended in divorce. Today money is the number one reason for fights in relationships.[54]

A good gauge when choosing to take a promotion or even change careers is to use a work-life balance formula like the one below.

Work-Life Balance = Quality of Life / Work Stress

Let's do the math, if a new job will cause an increase in Quality of Life (QoL) = 4, and Work Stress (WS) = 1, your Work-Life Balance (WLB) has the potential for a positive change up four-times better! Take that job! The benefits gained far outweigh the small increase in work stress.

---

[54] (Holland, 2015)

On the flip side, if you predict the change will increase your QoL=1 but increase your WS=4, your WLB has the potential to be affected negatively by 75%! If you do the math, even though you get a bump up in QoL, i.e., more money or prestige, it is overshadowed by the larger increase in WS. The negative effects of work stress outweigh the small increase in the promotion's benefits. In this case, at least to me, the money is not worth it.

This ideal is critical to enjoying your life. If a promotion is going to add one level to your Work Stress (WS=1), and one level to your Quality of Life (QoL=1), you'll make more money and maintain the Work-Life Balance (WLB) you're currently enjoying. To me, this is a smart opportunity, and I would take it. If WS goes up to (WS=5) and QoL goes up to (QoL=2), your WLB is diluted by .4 or 40%! This job will increase the suck of the grind by 40%.

The attitude of "living to work" is one I don't understand myself, but so many of my Gen X peers and Boomer friends still think this way. I live in an area where people have a relaxed, low-stress lifestyle. Adults pile six deep in golf carts and ride up to our town center and grab dinner and listen to live music or hit the marina for some oysters and reggae. I work so that I can enjoy the lifestyle of my choice and have a healthy work-life balance. Find the balance that works for you. Just make sure not to get too relaxed; we must all earn a living.

Note to Millennials and Gen Z: Just using the terms Work-Life Balance or Quality-of-Life can make older generations who may be workaholic prone, feel like the people who use the phrase are lazy or have a poor work ethic. Be careful to whom you are speaking when using these terms. Instead, use words and phrases such as; the company's wellness program, creating a positive workplace environment, or adding a company benefit. These are all palatable terms that can encompass everything needed to create a better work-life balance.

The Value of the Techno "Brain Gap"

There is one significant advantage that the Millennial mind brings to the team-building process and a team's ability to produce effective, efficient results. It is their orientation toward technology. The older generations see technology from an outsider's view looking in. They must adopt new ways of working with technology, while Millennials and Gen Z see technology as a part of their existence. It is a part of who they are and how they live. Neuroscientist Gary Small has studied the experience of growing up with technology. He has coined the phrase "brain gap" to refer to the differences in which the brains of Boomers and Gen Xers operate as opposed to those of Millennials.

Today's millennial generation has never known a world without technology. It is part of their everyday existence; it is how they connect with the world and others. Carol Bartz, in a 2009 article from The Economist states, "Today, new employees arrive on their first day with an alarming amount of know-it-all. They have already read about you, and the online critiques of your plans, strategies, and management style."[55] If that was the case in 2009, how much more is this true for today's new hires?

The propensity for technology has a positive effect on the ability to multitask, process visual information, and filtering

---

[55] (Bartz, 2009)

of information, however, it has left shortcomings in the areas of the brain used in face-to-face interactions.[56] There is a new importance on learning analytical business skills, understanding what data and information to gather, how to process and analyze it, and transform it into knowledge for sound decision making.

In contrast, Traditionalist and Baby Boomers learned to communicate in an analog world. Face-to-face, phone calls, written letters, policies, and memorandums are their preferred methods of communication. Gen X is stuck in the middle, with bosses who want face-to-face, phone, and written communications. Meanwhile, they have to lead teams of younger, tech-savvy professionals who want to use texts, company blogs, web-search, Twitter, and social networking to keep apprised of work-related activities. There is a double-tiered problem in middle management trying to communicate with Traditionalist and Baby Boomer senior managers, and then lead teams of Millennials into action.[57]

Disseminating information within the organization is also becoming more challenging. Most workers use email at work while texting is becoming more of a norm as a communication tool. However, outside of direct work activities, Millennials do not engage email as a primary communication tool between friends. They use email for contacting utility companies, ordering online, and other non-social communication. They also have more than one email address for different uses. Choosing online content

---

[56] (Hershatter & Epstein, 2010)
[57] (Taylor & Gao, 2014)

channels is particularly relevant to reaching them with mass distributed company information.

Many large corporations use blogs and other methods preferred by Millennials. Listening to digital marketing experts is the best way to learn how to communicate organizational messages to Millennials and Gen Z effectively. Studies by Pew Research give insight into generational engagement with online content. The percentage of each generation who believes the Internet makes life better is as follows, (Sorry Gen Z, Pew Research didn't have your data yet):

- 90% Millennials.
- 89 % Gen Xers.
- 89% Boomers.
- 78% Traditionalists.[58]

Hence, companies who are fully embracing blogs, website communication, and social media outlets are reaching their employees most effectively. With the proliferation of information, Millennials and Gen Z have a much broader and more diverse view of the world as compared to a much narrower view of the older generations. This is mostly due to the ease of access to globally diverse information.[59]

As a Boomer or Traditionalist, are you ready to make a change, if that change improves team effectiveness? Being efficient at an ineffective process makes no sense, yet I regularly see it in operational procedures. Go ahead and let the younger generations bring positive change. Then use

---

[58] (Jiang, 2018)
[59] (Jiang, 2018)

your practical wisdom to make these innovations efficient. What better partnership between generations could a company desire?!

The Value of Leisure Time

A prime example of the changing attitudes toward work and personal time is the way the generations view vacation and leisure. There is such a difference that travel companies are changing their marketing programs to target the types of trips preferred by Millennials.

In today's connected world, Millennials have a 23% greater desire to travel abroad than older generations, regardless of their stage in life[60], and make up 20% of all international travelers.[61] Their family, friends, and followers get to take part in the experience through their blogs, tweets, Instagram pics, Facebook posts, and other social media outlets.

I love to travel, and growing up, my family was more fortunate than others. As a Gen Xer and child of a Traditionalist, I was always amazed at the number of my high school friends who had never traveled outside our home state. Some had never been outside of our city! My father loved to take family vacations, and every year we would take a traditional American family trip. We would load up our land yacht, AKA, the Buschman family 'truckster,' and hit the highway. Depending on the year, our land yacht was either an Oldsmobile '88, Buick Electra 225 LTD, or Ford Country Square station wagon. There were no cell phones, no laptops, just the family. To pass the time, we played games like 'slug bug' and counted how many state

---

[60] (Barton, 2013)
[61] (Mya, 2017)

license plates we saw as we drove. I didn't fly on an airplane until I went on spring break as a sophomore in college and I paid for my plane ticket.

Listen to this Boomer's comments about vacation. "I didn't take a vacation for the first 15 years of my work career. My wife had to force me to take it for my health. I didn't even enjoy the first one. I felt guilty that I wasn't working. All I could think about was how I was letting my patients down by not being there for them." Feeling guilty for not working long hours is just a symptom of the society and time in which they grew up. The world was recovering from the devastation of WWII, and America was in the midst of the most substantial manufacturing growth period in its history. It was also a time where schools were conducting nuclear attack drills, the height of the Cold War, and people communicated face-to-face, and I don't mean through FaceTime.

Millennials and Gen Z, you must understand that this is how many Boomers feel; they feel guilty if they are not working. If you talk more about time off and your social life than work, Boomers are not going to like it, much less connect with you. Boomers are more likely to wait until five o'clock and then ask what people are doing after work. If you ask around, you will probably find out that many of your older co-workers have a place and time they get together once a week or so. As awkward as it may feel, try asking them face-to-face. They will respect you for this, and even if the place they go sucks, go anyway, this is how you build relationships.

Note to Millennials and Gen Z: Try starting up a conversation with those in leadership ranks above you about travel. The older generations are very proud and excited to share about their travels. When they were growing up, only affluent Americans traveled extensively, especially internationally. Vacationing was a sign that you had reached some level of achievement in life. Talking about them is a great relationship builder. Make sure not to hog the conversation with your stories. Let the other generations share more. Their exuberance to share is not out of disrespect or pride, remember they are just as excited as you about the ability to travel! Chances are, your experiences will have lots of commonalities and lots of differences that will enrich the conversation. You might even ask if any of them have stayed in a hostel in Europe and what they experienced.

Whether enjoying backpacking through Europe, African safaris, South American Carnival, or relaxing in the Caribbean, enjoying travel is a commonality among all generational leaders.

The Value of Collective Bargaining

I had the privilege to interview the owner and president of a small to medium business (SMB) who coded and sold software for communications companies. The president was a tech-savvy, Gen Xer. As I asked him about his company structure and how he related to his staff, he told me that most of his leaders were Millennials leading other Millennials. The exception was his sales team. He leads them personally because he built his company on his sales abilities.

He had ten salespeople, and he said they were all top performers; A players. There wasn't a B player in the bunch, much less a C player. However, one day, he had a meeting with them about changing their compensation plan. The team gave him no feedback during or after the session; they just listened to his ideas.

That Thursday, the team asked if they could have a meeting with the president on Friday. He set up the meeting and asked his team to lead it. In the meeting, the team told him they had collectively decided if he changed the compensation plan; they would all resign! He was shocked, in all his Gen X days, he would have never thought white-collar collective bargaining may enter the workforce, much less in his company!

The president didn't want to lose his team, they were performing well, and the damage to the company would have been severe, so he thanked them for their feedback, and suggested the next time something like this came up, they should tell him their thoughts upfront. He cares about their opinion. He could have avoided this by getting their feedback and ideas before mentioning in passing he was considering the changes. He should have held an Appreciative Inquiry (AI) meeting first and allowed them to "share and care." We'll talk more about AI later.

Communication is essential if we want to understand each other and avoid situations like this one or worse. When forward-thinking, creative Gen X leaders ask for your input, they truly want it. The idea of white-collar collective bargaining is strange and outside the box for all the older generations, including Gen X. However, if people genuinely are the corporation, what rights do they or should they have? Whether stockholder, management, white-collar, or blue-collar employee? Let's consider the point a little deeper. Is it an employee's right to negotiate employment contracts as part of the free market system, whether individually or collectively? The exchange of talents and time for remuneration and benefits received from the company is what's negotiated. So, could white-collar collective bargaining be more purely capitalistic than traditionally thought? Could be!

The idea lends itself to the concept of democracy in the workplace as well; however, the workplace is one of the long-standing hold outs to democratic leadership. Infusing democracy into organizational leadership has been a focus of the Organization Development (OD) practice since the 1950s. In Europe, the idea of democratically run corporations has caught on in many countries. Germany, who has one of the strongest manufacturing economies in the world, has collective bargaining rights built into its nation's constitution. OD is proving that companies that use democratic principles and strategies to manage and lead are attaining new levels of effectiveness and efficiency on global scales.

Maybe another source for the idea of white-collar collective bargaining is the growing number of blue-collar workers whose children have college degrees and are entering the white-collar workforce? Perhaps the widening concern about white-collar workplace conditions has nothing to do with a perceived lack of work ethic; maybe it's something completely different and better? Either way, tread very carefully regarding suggesting changes in your workplace, as you don't want to get labeled as a complainer, which would be a career-limiting move (CLM). Present new ideas as positive additions to the workplace. If there is a cost, be prepared to show a justification for benefits to the company.

The Value of Being a Company Man

A national program manager, who had a comfortable six-figure income, was having a conversation with his VP, who was a Gen Xer. He told his boss that he came to work to support his lifestyle and the things he enjoyed outside of work. The VP promptly moved the conversation into his office, closed the door, and asked, "Is everything ok? Are you thinking about resigning or going to a competitor?" When the manager repeated his statement, the VP said, "In my MBA program, I learned there is something wrong with a person whose motive for working was to support their own needs and lifestyle. The professors said not to hire such a person, and if one of my staff made that sort of statement, there was something seriously wrong. We work for the company's betterment, not our own."

Wow! Wow! Wow! What a statement!! "We are supposed to work for the company's betterment and not our own?!" Many Boomers and Gen Xers still feel this way about "being a company man" and that they "serve the company" as if it had personhood or was a living entity. It is true that we should put the company's wellbeing and success at the top of our list, but not at the cost of doing harm to or forgetting about ourselves. Our skills in the marketplace have value. In Germany, worker's rights are written into their constitution. Looking at how German and Northern European workers interact with their employers can provide positive lessons on finding a balance between making a profit and doing good for employees.

Where did this idea that a corporation has a persona come from? To understand this phenomenon, we must go back to 1886. At that time, the Supreme Court of the United States declared that corporations are "persons" just like you and I are persons and have the same rights as American citizens. This decision extended the protections of the 14th Amendment to include corporations, giving them personhood! The reasoning behind their conclusion is that corporations consist of a group of people. Since these people have rights, those rights extend to the incorporated entity.

Stockholders are the legal group of people that are members of a corporation. Therefore, our forefathers were enabled to look at non-stockholding employees as servants for hire. Eventually, this viewpoint dehumanized workers and removed emotion and compassion from leadership. It allowed workers to be thought of no differently than a truck, desk, or widget. The employees were to serve the stockholders and the corporation.

You should be getting a feel for how Traditionalists, Boomers, and many Gen Xers came to think about work. When you, Millennial or Gen Z, express corporations are responsible to its employees to provide safe, healthy working conditions, health care, and treat its employees with civility and fairness, you are going against 100 years of legally and socially ingrained thinking. However, these ideals have been in flux for centuries, and you can bring change. Things are changing, and other nations have recognized the benefits of meeting workers' needs. If you are going to bring change, please make sure to do it positively.

The progressive Gen Xers and most Millennials I've spoken to believe that corporations consist of the shareholders and the people who work for it. When leadership empowers its workforce and sets it free from extraneous, outdated workplace rules and norms, it allows them to excel, and in return, the employees are loyal and work harder.

Gen Z, Millennials, and forward-thinking Gen Xers are saying, "Give us the freedom we were promised under the 14th Amendment to pursue life, liberty, and happiness in the workplace, without the encumbrances that hampered our parents' generations. Let us succeed apart from workplace traditions when those traditions suppress our abilities and freedom to perform our jobs in today's connected society." They are demanding the rights afforded them by the US Constitution and Supreme Court; what a different way to think about and consider the actions and work ethic of a Millennial. They are rebels and patriots! I love it!! Two leadership theories that support these freedoms are Transformational and Servant-Based Leadership.

The Value of Career Choice

On the first day of every undergraduate class I teach, I start my classes out with a lesson in "Why." Why are the students there in the first place? As a group we scratch out cost of living information on the whiteboards and discuss how much it costs to live as a single person. What level of income does it take if you want to have a place of your own, a decent car, pay utilities, and still have some spending money left over? What is terrifying, unless the student is already on their own, virtually none of the students have a clue how much it will take to support themselves. We then discuss their value in the job market, how every role has a salary range or hourly rate range for which a hiring manager and human resources (HR) can offer them, and that each skill has monetary value in the job market. My goal is for them to understand why they are there. They are in class to add capabilities to be able to command a premium in the employment market and start a career. The more valuable their skills and skill level, the more likely they will be able to choose a role within a company and set the direction of their career themselves.

However, I also explain that money, job status, and lots of spending cash doesn't guarantee a happy life. America is the most affluent society in history, yet one in six adults takes some form of anti-depressant or prescribed psychiatric medicine.[62] So what's missing? One thing that can help with a person's quality of life and their work-life balance, is learning how to choose a career and not just get a job. There are typically three steps I teach my students so that they can tailor their bachelor's degree accordingly.

Already have a degree or job? You can follow these steps at any point in your life. Asking these questions multiple times throughout your career and life will be helpful. Doing some soul searching along life's journey, especially after major events like getting married and having kids, can identify new needs and reasons for a change. It might even help keep you from finding yourself stuck in a job or industry you don't like.

1. Step one is to take an inventory of the things you like to do. What is it that you enjoy? Choose one that has a business connection. For instance, if you love to hunt, you might consider working for a manufacturing company that makes outdoor gear.

2. The second step is to ask yourself, are you good at it? You must have an aptitude in the area. We've all seen contestants on TV singing shows, who love to sing, but when they open their mouths, what comes

---

[62] (Bogdan, 2016)

out sounds like a wailing animal, right? If you're tone-deaf, you're more than likely not going to be good at singing. Choose something you enjoy doing and for which you have the aptitude.

3. The third step is to go to a website such as GlassDoor.com or Salary.com and find out which positions pay the most, and which companies have the highest employee ratings. Pick out a few roles that sound good and go to each companies' career sites and check out the requirements required to fill the position.

4. Finally, get trained. The description of the role will have the hiring criteria and skill requirements listed. What more could we ask? Each company clearly states what they are looking for; now, it is your role to get qualified.

If you want to work in Information Technology (IT), you might consider getting an MCSE, CCNA, or Cyber Security certification to go along with your bachelor's in computer science, and so forth. The older a person gets, the more complicated this change becomes, but for those who have made the change, they say it's been well worth the effort. It has been for me.

If you follow these or similar steps, hopefully, you will be employed in a career and not just a job. You will be able to do what you like, in a position you enjoy, and make the amount of money that you choose, whatever that may be. Just make sure it will pay for the lifestyle you want to live. I need to add a disclaimer that the hiring process is never guaranteed, no matter how qualified the person. These steps do not guarantee a job, a career, or that you will be happy in your employment or life. However, following them can at least give you a shot at a good start or a positive mid-life career change.

The Value of Change and Innovation

The Traditionalist generation is called that for a reason. They are the link between the generations before them, who lived in an era when changes came at a snail's pace, and the generations who grew up in the fast-moving age of technology. For hundreds even thousands of years, traditions passed from generation to generation. However, with the advancement of equality, personal liberty, and political freedom, we are learning that not all those traditions were healthy or right, just ask Ambedkar and Dewey! If you are not sure who these gentlemen were, Dewey[63] was a professor at Columbia University. Dewey's philosophies were very influential in how the U.S. educational system developed and the learning environment Millennials and Gen Z students experienced. He was also responsible for much of the Reconstructionist Theory. Ambedkar, one of Dewey's students from India, picked up where Gandhi left off and brought massive change to India. He confronted caste systems in India and helped the untouchables gain social acceptance. Ambedkar also authored India's constitution. He accomplished these feats by helping convince the nation's leaders that some traditions were good and others were harmful. It is the responsibility of the current generation to strain out harmful cultural norms, protect those in their care, and institute new practices when needed.[64]

---

[63] (Dewey, 1916, 1944, 1997)
[64] (Ambedkar, 1936, 1937, 1944, 2018)

Dewey was a pragmatist, as am I. A pragmatist believes that you must put theory to practice and see if it works. If it doesn't work, try something else! Dewey pointed out the fact that not all traditions are good, some are harmful, such as the caste system in India, which both Gandhi and later Ambedkar[65], tried to annihilate. Dewey also points out that as society changes, historical traditions and norms that were once good may become harmful in the present time.[66] Holding on to destructive ideas like bigotry, sexual harassment, distrust of other cultures, races, and ages, leads to statements like, "I just don't get those young people. I don't like their music, their hair, the way they talk, or their attitudes!" In America, the older generations seem to criticize the younger generations, and the younger ones rebel against their elders. It's our "American tradition," and we wonder why our children rebel against our leadership, and leadership treats younger people with disdain. Let's stop the insanity and try something new!

Let's reach out and learn some advanced leadership skills that work for all generations! Maybe we'll find out we're not that different after all, and that many leadership skills are timeless while others are not. Let's embrace healthy leadership traditions and replace unhealthy, harmful ones.

---

[65] (Ambedkar, 1936, 1937, 1944, 2018)
[66] (Dewey, 1916, 1944, 1997)

Reflections

Take five minutes and reflect on what you've learned. Write down at least three takeaways. At the end of the book you will have 30+ key ideas to review that will help mold your thinking, build bridges, and bolster your leadership skills.

1._____

_____

_____

_____

_____

_____

2._____

_____

_____

_____

_____

3._____

_____

_____

_____

_____

_____

_____

_____

_____

_____

Chapter 4: What is Leadership

Managing is not Enough

An RVP is consulting with his regional manager (RM) and a director. The RVP has an opening on his staff and wants their advice on a couple of internal candidates. Both candidates are performing well in their positions, which, of course, is an essential requirement. They both have the industry knowledge and have proven that they can lead their teams successfully, so this is going to be a tough decision. Both candidates' skills, education, and performance are equivalent. The RVP asks, "If you had to report to one or the other, who would you choose and why?" The regional manager answered, "Candidate A, because not only does she already have good relationships with our leadership team, she has a strong voice." The director asked, "What do you mean by a strong voice?" The RM responded, "She can stand on her own two feet, doesn't allow others to bully her, when she states her opinion it's based on fact, not emotion, and it's defendable. She also doesn't provoke or point fingers at other leaders. If the group goes with her idea, that's great, and if they don't, she accepts the decision and then executes the leadership team's plan. As I said, she has a strong voice, and her 360-degree review reflects that". The director chimed in, "I get it, and you're right; she has the respect of everyone around her, and candidate B doesn't have her kind of voice. He hasn't shown the confidence to lead at this level in challenging situations without buckling under pressure." The RVP thanked them and hired Candidate A.

For years organizations have tried to answer these questions:

- What are the differences between a leader and a manager?
- Can managers be leaders?
- If so, what qualities would make them a leader? If not, why?
- What traits, characteristics, and behaviors make a good leader, and why is this so important?

Being able to identify and hire leaders can make the difference between thriving as a business, barely making a profit, or going out of business. Managers are put in place to manage a preexisting process. Managers manage a process or people to meet the status quo, industry averages, or a current target. It is their job to ensure that tasks get done. However, getting tasks done doesn't always mean a manager is doing the right things. Many managers can be completely disengaged from the workplace yet manage their team to a number or goal. However, they may have no drive to excel or find better ways of doing business. Finding ways to excel and doing business better are examples of doing the right things. Leaders work and think in ways that help prepare and position their companies for long-term growth and success. They must be innovators and forward thinkers.

What is Leadership?

First, let's define leadership. **Leadership is a process by which an individual influences a group or team to accomplish a set of goals.**[67] The person doing the influencing is, of course, the leader. However, there are two other elements to

---

[67] (Hughes & Ginnett, 2015)

consider; the leader must first build a team of followers and then influence them, so they successfully perform within a specific set of circumstances. So then, both their team and the marketplace circumstances, are critical factors in how successful a leader may be and how the leader uses different strategies to influence others.

Many organizations and emerging leaders make the mistake of thinking the leader is the only important part of the leadership equation. However, circumstances and the peculiarities and traits of those following are equal determining factors of a leader's success. Considering every person and situation is different, leaders must learn to use a variety of strategies, actions, and behaviors. Three essential areas critical to leadership success are:

- Leadership skills, competency, and education.
- Experience on the job.
- Knowledge of their business and industry.

Human resource departments and hiring senior executives look at potential leadership candidates and evaluate their prowess in each of these three areas. An experienced sales executive who has in-depth knowledge of their industry, but no training or education as a leader will most likely fail. Likewise, an MBA graduate with no experience or industry knowledge most likely will not succeed. Leadership candidates should have a balance in all three of these areas.

Note to Emerging Leaders: As you apply for and seek after leadership positions, make sure to cover your strengths in each of these areas on your résumé, during your interview, and especially when meeting face-to-face with the hiring team. Show them you are a good fit for the role and highlight the value your skills in these areas bring. Also, be prepared to address your weaknesses. We'll discuss handling skill gaps later.

Leadership Theories You Need to Know

Written leadership theory has its roots in philosophy dating back to the ancient people groups of the Hebrews, Phoenicians, Greeks, and Romans. One early written record we have of an organization's operational structure is when Moses was experiencing what appeared to be leadership burn out. Moses sought advice from his father- in-law who told him the wise thing to do. Take his best leaders and put them over groups of 1000, then identify the second-best leaders and put them in charge of groups of 100 people, and finally, a third tier who would be over groups of 10. History records this as the first written organization hierarchy design. Of course, we know that leadership structures existed in earlier times, but from a written record, this is the earliest organizational design.

Take notice of which theories each generation experienced in school, college, and at work. Seek insight as to how each generation may view leadership.

- **1513 A.D.: Machiavellian Leadership.** Uses selfish manipulation to reach goals, reasoning that the end justifies the means. Does not consider moral right or wrong.[68]

- **350 B.C. – 1800s: The Great Man Theory.** Leaders are born. Only certain people have the natural ability to lead. Established in ancient Greece and

---

[68] (Schaeffer, 2018)

72

Roman Empires, prevailed through the Dark Ages up till the 18th century.

- **1800s: The Trait Theory of Leadership.** Distinct trait characteristics determine successful leaders. However, all leadership situations are different, and researchers found dozens of aspects that were situation dependent.

- **1947: Transactional Theory of Leadership.** Rewarding compliance and punishing non-compliance. Also known as carrot and stick or manage by objective (MBO) method.

- **1955: The Skills Theory of Leadership.** To get people to follow you, you need interpersonal, tech, and conceptual skills. Be good at what you do, have superb relationship skills, and be a visionary; see the big picture.

- **1958: The Contingency Theory of Leadership.** Different situations require different leadership styles. The right leader must be matched with the right situation.

- **1964: The Style Theory of Leadership.** Uses different styles as needed, such as autocracy (demanding), democratic (let others participate), laissez-faire (hands-off), and team management (equally concerned for people and performance, Blake and Mouton's Managerial Grid).

- **1969: The Situational Theory of Leadership.** Different situations require different styles, and leaders must adapt.

- **1970s: Leader-Member Exchange Theory of Leadership.** Relational leadership in which leaders have a close relationship with those they lead and those they choose to mentor as apprentices. It creates an atmosphere of an "in-group" and an "out-group."

- **1970: Servant-Based Theory of Leadership.** By identifying and fulfilling the follower's needs, it builds an atmosphere of trust, cooperation, and reciprocal appreciation and performance. People follow out of gratitude versus fear, coercion, or compulsion. It dates back to the 1st century.

- **1973: Transformational Theory of Leadership.** Cultivates followers by being concerned with personal and professional development. Identifies areas where individuals and teams need to change to accomplish their goals. Uses motivation and inspiration to guide followers and to produce effective outcomes.[69]

- **2000s: Emerging Theories of Leadership.** Emerging theories combine aspects of other approaches and believe there is no one best theory. New breeds of leadership theory taking shape are relational and positive psychology based, innovative, and creative leadership approaches. These theories posit that

---

[69] (Zigarelli, 2013)

74

leaders must be multi-dimensional and lead through innovation and creativity to navigate today's volatile, uncertain, complex, and ambiguous (VUCA) business world.[70]

Note to All: YouTube search; "Ten Leadership Theories in Five Minutes." You will find short summaries of them.[71]

What Does Leadership Mean to You?

To become a new or advancing leader, we must recognize that generational differences are evident in various leadership styles. The differences in "attitudes, values, and beliefs of the generational cohorts are believed to influence how each generation views leadership, which then manifests itself in the use of different preferred leadership styles."[72] Boomers choose a mutual and consensual method through communication and sharing responsibility; Gen Xers lean toward egalitarian ideals and have little respect for authority. However, Gen Xers put a high value on honesty, fairness, competence, and straightforwardness. Millennials prefer the respectful dynamics of influence, collaboration, and expect their leaders to bring it together.[73] Millennials desire interaction with leaders and want to apply their knowledge and skills. They want to have direct access to leadership and use dialogue to facilitate change.[74]

Each generation was exposed to different views of leadership. Table 1 should help you think about what goes

---

[70] (Livingston, 2014)
[71] (Zigarelli, 2013)
[72] (Zemke, Raines, & Filipczak, 2013)
[73] (Sessa, Kabacoff, Deal, & Brown, 2007)
[74] (Hinote & Sundvall, 2015)

through your head versus other generations' when it comes to thinking about leadership. Where do you fall in the mix?

- Traditionalist: Born 1928-1945.
- Baby Boomers: Born 1946-1964.
- Gen X: Born 1965-1980.
- Millennials: Born 1981-1996.
- Gen Z: Born 1997-2012.

	Traditional	Boomer	Gen X	Millennial	Gen Z
The Great Man	X	X	X	X	X
Machiavellian	X	X	X	X	X
Trait Theory	X	X	X	X	X
Transaction	X	X	X	X	X
Skills Theory		X	X	X	X
Contingency		X	X	X	X
Style Theory			X	X	X
Situational			X	X	X
Leader-Member			X	X	X
Servant				X	X
Transform				X	X
Emergent/ Innovative					X

Table 1: Exposure to Leadership Theories

Think about how your peers, followers, and superiors view leadership. If you are a younger leader, older leaders may not understand the concepts you believe in the most. To connect with, follow, or lead them, you must begin to use emotional intelligence, cultural intelligence, and positive interpersonal relationship skills. If you don't, the different generations will tend to resist becoming your followers.

Note to All: Please take a few minutes and reflect on yourself and your humanity; what is in you is in them; human desires, traits, and ideas. Contemplate how the different leadership theories each generation has experienced have shaped their ideas about leadership. Use the understanding that comes from this short reflection exercise to help shape how you lead. Communicate in a leadership language that includes attitudes, words, and actions they will understand.

What Makes a Competent Leader?

Competent leaders build teams and have long term results, thereby leading their teams and companies to sustainable high performance. Studies show that only 25% of leaders in corporate America are competent. That means 75% of corporate leaders land somewhere between competent and incompetent.[75] Incompetent leaders have varying degrees of success and failure and can be separated into four broad leadership styles:

- Country Club: Get limited results but have happy employees.
- Impoverished: Get limited results, are disengaged managers, and have unhappy employees.
- Produce-or-Perish: Get short-term, unsustainable results and have unhappy employees.
- Middle of the Road: Get average results and have marginally happy employees.

---

[75] (Hughes & Ginnett, 2015)

Managing stress levels well and knowing your numbers are good leadership qualities. However, without combining them with team-building skills, they produce insufficient or short-term results and thereby are considered incompetent leadership styles.

Note to All: Try using Blake and Mouton's Managerial Grid[76] to locate yourself and the leaders for whom you work. Having sincere care for people and a thorough concern for results produces high-performance and long-term success.

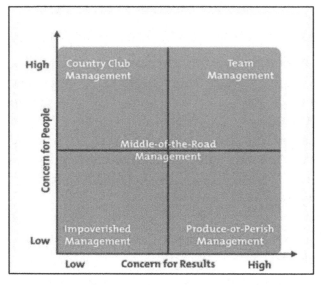

Figure 1: Blake and Mouton's Managerial Grid.[77]

Intelligence, Personality, and Values

Research confirms that certain personality traits can predict leadership potential, but the potential is not enough. Leaders are not born; they're made. The qualities and characteristics

---

[76] (Mind Tools, n.d.)
[77] (Blake & McCanse, 1991)

which may predict if you have the potential to become a good leader are distinguishable, and you can test yourself and others for them.[78] The three foundational areas in which to look for the building blocks of potential leadership are:

- Personal Intelligence.
- Personality Type/Leadership Maturity.
- Personal/Corporate Values.

Academic performance and highest educational degree achieved typically measures a person's level of intelligence. Hard skills, which are tangible skills such as accounting, economics, financial modeling, and industry-specific expertise, can also be documented by obtaining industry certifications and completing training programs. Formal education, performing well in one's current role, and taking advantage of company-sponsored education programs is vital.

The second foundational block is a person's personality type and leadership maturity level. These are essential components of developing soft skills. Soft skills are concerned with the psychological and interpersonal interaction aspects of leadership. A person's soft skill proficiency is significantly affected by their personality type and level of leadership maturity. One of the best systems to identify your personality type is the Enneagram[79] test. Virginia Price, Ph.D. developed the Enneagram, while completing her doctorate at Harvard Business School. To find your level of leadership maturity, use the

---

[78] (Hughes & Ginnett, 2015)
[79] (Daniels & Price, 2009)

methodologies in Maureen Metcalf and Mark Palmer's, *"Innovative Leadership Fieldbook."*[80] These two resources link personality types and levels of leadership maturity together and provide exercises, that if practiced, build on strengths and shore up weaknesses.

Personality type and leadership maturity level have nothing to do with age, experience, or time spent in a management position. Not all people mature to higher levels of leadership maturity, and likewise, not all people overcome their personality trait weaknesses. You can gain great insight into yourself using these two tools. They will help increase your level of leadership maturity and overcome personality shortcomings.

Another personality test is the DISC test, which Tony Robbins[81] uses. Considering the age and current studies commenting on the effectiveness of the Myers and Briggs personality test, I would choose the Enneagram test and the *"Innovative Leadership Fieldbook"* strategies hands down.

The third foundational block is "leadership fit." How well do you mesh with and fit into the leadership team and corporate culture? We are all familiar with having to fit into groups in social and cultural settings. Still many times, we don't consider that every organization has its own cultural and social workplace vibe.

Sometimes, we just don't fit into a company's culture, and that's ok because if you have leadership aptitude, eventually, you will find a place where you do. When advising people

---

[80] (Metcalf & Palmer, 2011)
[81] (Tony Robbins, 2019)

who are in a career search, I always tell them to visit a company's website, social media, and look up reviews on the work environment and leaders to get a feel for the company. If you are genuinely looking for a career, you're going to want to work for a company where you enjoy the work environment and the work. Otherwise, you'll end up merely landing another job you don't enjoy, and even if you're a top performer, you'll eventually leave due to dissatisfaction. I can vouch for that.

High-Performance Leaders

Who are high-performance leaders? **Leaders have formal power and responsibilities; high-performing leaders are people of influence.** Research at Cornell University indicates that effective, successful leaders are those with strong character and the ability to lead with courage, humility, and compassion.[82]

High performers do not lead like average leaders, and they do not just manage processes. If a company forces them to conform to a leadership mold meant to fit into a corporate box neatly, they will become frustrated and leave. Stifling a creative, innovative leader, demoralizes them and strips them of the very powers that made them great. Forced conformity in today's fast-moving and constantly shifting marketplace, suffocates growth, and produces missed opportunities. Allowing room for creativity and originality will help unlock the potential of high-performing leaders.

High-performing leaders are equally passionate about their team members' well-being and meeting performance goals. If we as leaders expect or demand more from our teams than

---

[82] (Cornell University, 2019)

what we are willing to reciprocate in mentoring, coaching, guidance, training, and compensation, then our leadership is out of balance.

Companies are a complex mix of people in social interactions and relationships at work. These interactions drive all work. The stronger and better managed they are, the more effective and productive a company will be. Distancing yourself personally and emotionally from your team promotes employee disengagement and work complacency. Unfeeling, cold, uncaring managers force their teams into compliance using coercive power as opposed to leading their teams to success using influential, relational, and referent powers. Be a leader; learn to motivate people. As Eric Trist said, "No one can force change on anyone else."[83]

As a leader, ask yourself, "Do I crave to be served and supported more than I desire to support and build up my team?" High-performing leaders desire to build up their teams more than their desire for personal achievement.

Change Resistant Leaders

A regional manager hired to transform a faltering systems analyst team joined his first executive conference call. When introduced as having a master's degree in information systems, the SVP of Sales commented, "I don't know what that brings to the table?" Within one year, the regional manager transformed the team into the company's second-highest revenue producer by introducing innovative, creative, and leading practices from outside the industry. The regional manager understood change and how to

---

[83] (Davy & Harris PhD, 2005)

manage it. His team was positioned with the company's change initiatives and the need to rapidly respond to market conditions. The company implemented the processes he and his team perfected on a national scale. Yet when leaders from corporate HQ asked who was responsible, his boss and another senior leader took credit for his work. These regional executive managers saw no need to change or to embrace those with formal educations. They did not genuinely agree with their corporate leaders and became resistant leaders.

To protect themselves, the resistant leaders formed a coalition and surrounded those who were bringing change. They either converted them to the dark side or pushed them down or out of the company. Over the next three years, the company hemorrhaged talent, and only other resistant leaders at headquarters knew it. The regional senior managers had become experts at protecting their jobs and keeping change out. Change, even positive change, was their enemy. Their skillsets were stale, and the company performance slowed, resulting in several reorganizations and RIFs. It also cost the president of field operations his job. Resistant leadership is a sly thief.

The senior leaders from corporate headquarters could have used the amoeba management strategy to identify and deal with resistant leaders. Instead, the resistant leaders used the strategy in reverse to protect themselves and push their agendas. The amoeba approach divides a company into smaller parts, and each team leader is responsible for their division. Reward systems are adjusted to support the changes, and through collaboration and cooperation, the divisional leaders implement the executive team's plans. **When leaders agree with the corporate direction, divisional**

leaders can surround those who are resisting it. Through coaching, reorganization, reductions in force, and other means, resistant leaders are either transformed, absorbed, or exited. To get an understanding, take a few moments and watch a YouTube clip on how an amoeba surrounds its food and absorbs it.

The effect of the amoeba strategy can be positive or negative. When used to make a positive, forward-moving change, it is a highly efficient way to transform or consume divisions and managers who are resistant to change. When used negatively, the results are what happened to the regional manager and company in the example above. Several factors that cause and spread resistance to change are personal ambition, cohesion and collaboration among leaders who disagree with the corporate direction, lack of change management, and insufficient leadership education.[84] **Resistant leadership results when personal achievement outweighs the commitment to team and organization development.**

One consequence of resistant leadership is that organizations will not produce at optimal, long-term, and sustainable levels. Baby Boomers and Gen Xers become less engaged, and younger generations avoid working under these conditions. Only low and mid-level talent will put up with it; those who have nowhere else to go or are too afraid to change companies will stay on board. The worst outcome is that the highly compensated senior managers will keep getting paid, up to the day the company realizes their change or growth initiative has failed.

---

[84] (Inamori, 2013)

As an old friend of mine once told me when we worked for resistant leadership, "Everyone who can leave this place has left. I'd start looking for an exit plan." and I did. This friend was one of the best leaders for which I have worked. He went on to hold a global role at a better company, and then founded and sold his own technology company and is a millionaire today.

Keep in mind the longer resistance persists, the worse the effects will be. More and more quality people will seek employment elsewhere. Sooner or later, the loss of talent will become clear. **"Originality is the one thing which unoriginal minds cannot feel the use of," said John Stuart Mill.**[85] Agile, nimble, and creative leaders prize originality.

---

[85] (Mill, 2002)

Reflections

Take five minutes and reflect on what you've learned. Write down at least three takeaways. At the end of the book you will have 30+ key ideas to review that will help mold your thinking, build bridges, and bolster your leadership skills.

1._____

_____

_____

_____

_____

_____

2._____

_____

_____

_____

_____

_____

3._____

_____

_____

_____

_____

_____

_____

_____

_____

_____

_____

_____

Chapter 5: Getting on the Leadership Team

If you want to get on the leadership team or move up the leadership ranks, it might be a good idea to understand how organizations choose and promote their leaders. Current leaders and their human resource departments have a process of identifying and hiring leaders. Internal candidates are endorsed by those they work with and for, external candidates are referred through networking or identified through recruiting searches conducted by human resource (HR) departments. Either way, to vet potential leaders, there are necessary steps. This chapter seeks to provide you with some inside information on that process.

HR departments have specific requirements and a set of traits they look for when hiring for management positions. The basic requirement formulas vet out people without fundamental leadership skills. The requirements also provide a set of skills for new leadership candidates to learn before they apply. However, if a hiring decision is made using just these formulas, it can be catastrophic. As we've been discussing, being a leader is far more involved than just managing a business process and basic formulas can't decipher how to build dynamic leadership teams. If a company hires candidates with the same leadership DNA, i.e., similar personalities, strengths, and weaknesses, this may create corporate blindness. Hiring leaders with differing leadership DNA is vital to keep the organization strong and healthy. Heck, even Prince William and Prince Harry of the British royal family, are widening the family gene pool, as did their father when he married Princess Diana. Now the family has strong, healthy heirs that are growing the royal family baby by baby. Prince Harry is following in his mother's footsteps and reaching out to help meet people's needs and changing things up a bit. He's protecting his wife and family, while serving the Queen and kindling the nation's love for the Crown and its rulers!

Asking for an Advancement Opportunity

A friend of mine, who is a Millennial, and a leader, became VP of Sales by the time he was 30 years. He's now 38 and is considered a senior leader in his firm. In his first year with the company, he had a solid performance and felt like he "deserved some recognition." At that time, the "Great Recession," was in full swing, and even though he had a strong year, the company had not. In addition, his boss was working on making sure the company was profitable so he could keep his job. Regardless of the business climate (recession) and the fact that he was the FNG, he thought to himself, "I deserve a raise and probably a promotion" and asked his boss for both. Fortunately, he had a great boss who held back and didn't say what he was thinking. He then coached my friend, walking him through what he had just asked until he could see it from a leadership perspective and had an aha moment! He immediately realized the CLM he had made. He was incredibly grateful that he had a caring mentor for a boss.

If you are a solid performer, have leadership skills, and are ambitious, sometime around the two to three-year mark, you should be asking your supervisor about leadership opportunities. It will take that long for a company to trust that you are not a job hopper. If the company sees your potential, they will get you started in the leadership process. However, if they tell you they're interested but don't get you started in a development process, I would question their sincerity. If at the five-year mark, your company has shown no interest in promoting you, they do not believe you are leadership material, and you can plan on spending the rest of your life in the same role if you don't make a change.

Note to Millennials and Gen Z: One of the quickest ways to get yourself eliminated from being a leadership candidate is to be a job hopper. If you have changed jobs more than every three years, you better have a damn good reason or forget being considered. Under normal circumstances, no one will risk hiring or promoting you. Why would a company risk putting you in a leadership position and spend $30,000 to $60,000 training you to have you jump ship and disrupt their business flow? Then they must find another leader and start all over. Businesses that pay well and have good working conditions are smarter than that.

Knowledge, Skills, and Abilities

In the last chapter, we discussed what leadership is and the qualities and traits that a leader should have. They are the skills and foundational blocks that human resources (HR) will vet in the first stage of evaluating a leadership candidate. During this initial stage, expect phone interviews, online evaluation tools, video interviews, and maybe a couple of face-to-face meetings with HR or an initial applicant screener. Many large companies use taped video interviews, which HR uses to evaluate multiple aspects of an applicant. Make sure to practice your presentation(s) beforehand.

If you pass the first stage, you will become a candidate for leadership; in other words, they believe you possess the three foundational building blocks. At this point, you will move to the next qualification round. The first step in this next stage picks up where the initial stage ended and explores more deeply a candidate's fit for the specific position and the organization's values and culture. There must be a fit between the role, the organizational culture, and the potential leader's knowledge, skills, and abilities (KSAs).

Note to Emerging Leaders: If HR brings you in and has you meet with four or five people on the same day, they like you for the role. You're most likely the number one or two candidate. Leaders won't waste other's time having them interview you if they don't really like you. If they introduce you around the office, things are looking good.

If you get to this point and the process ends here, ask where you fell short and ask for a suggested possible course of action so that you can better prepare for the next opportunity. There's nothing to lose, your aptitude can only grow, and at a minimum, you'll do a better job next time. Becoming more proficient in the basic building blocks can be done!

If you or a potential leader are a fit and an internal candidate, conducting a 360-degree review is likely. The process involves your peers, superiors, and subordinates completing an anonymous survey about your skills and their experiences with you. The report provides a detailed look at your leadership strengths and weaknesses, how well they may match the role, and how you compare to the other candidates. A gap analysis for each candidate might follow to qualify and quantify your KSAs.

Gap Analysis Tips:

- A leadership candidate's knowledge and skillset should be current.

- Candidates should have a favorable attitude toward continuing education.
- Experience alone is not a good indication if a person will be successful.
- Experience doesn't equal ability. Many managers are incompetent for years.
- Now is the time to become competent and develop a reputation as an emerging leader.
- The evaluation of soft skills is a critical success factor.
- Start practicing emotional and cultural intelligence from day one.

Conducting a gap analysis of your current knowledge, skills/competencies, and abilities against those needed for a leadership role is a good practice. It will help identify your strengths and weaknesses. Where weaknesses exist, do something about them. If a requirement is an MBA, get one, it will change your life forever! Matching a candidate to a position is much like building a puzzle, make sure you have all the pieces and know where each one fits!

Companies that hire and promote people who are the same will end up creating a leadership team with no checks and balances, ending in organizational blindness or corporate psychosis. Bring this point to light. Human resource departments should monitor the skillsets and traits of each leader. Thinking that is focused on valuing every team member, will help keep leaders humble and be appreciative of those who surround them.

Continuous Improvement Mindset and Grit

Unfortunately, many people fail to keep their skillsets and business knowledge current. A leader must help guide a company into the future; stale skillsets and knowledge bases prevent them from doing so. If you have strong foundational leadership abilities, knowledge, and skills, improve them, and keep them updated. Showing a proven track record of continuing education and a motivation to learn applies to current and emerging leaders.

There is a grit factor in leadership. Make sure to take situational circumstances into consideration. Remember, the best leaders may not be the ones with the highest numbers; the best leaders are usually the ones who have successfully led their team to positive results through adverse and difficult situations. As a part of my doctoral studies, I wrote a research paper on how to measure and predict a person's ability to learn to lead. In my measurement grid, I included what I called a grit factor. The grit factor scored how difficult the circumstances were for a person to rise to their current position. Others may call this the "silver spoon" factor. Did they face adversity and overcome it, or was their path easy? Did they get a head start in life, or did they come from a disadvantaged background? Those who overcome adverse situations, develop stamina and grit. In academics, we call this rigor. Doctoral programs are incredibly rigorous. It is why only 4.5% of American's earn them, and that's up from the historic amount of 2%.[86]

Overcoming adversity and challenging circumstances is crucial to the development of a leader's character and

---

[86] (America Counts Staff, 2019)

perseverance. Will they stand with you in tough times, abandon ship, or give up? Will they be able to make the hard decisions that come with leadership responsibility? Google "grit factor" and check out the results. Organizations are discovering that tenacity is a success factor in leadership. Ask a successful entrepreneur, and they will tell you the same. Even college entrance exams, such as the ACT, are adding, a "grit" factor to their assessments. Below are some interesting statistics on the increasing levels of academic achievement from the United States Census Bureau. The current status of formal education and those who are achieving undergraduate and advanced degrees are:

- 35.2% of native-born Americans have a bachelor's degree or higher.
- 38.8% of immigrants who have arrived since 2000 have a bachelor's degree or higher.
- 38.4% of naturalized citizens have a bachelor's degree or higher.
- 39.6% of the children of immigrants have at least a bachelor's degree.
- Overall, 48.2% of Americans have a bachelor's degree, 21% have a master's degree, 3.2 % have a professional degree, and 4.5% have a doctorate.[87]

In 2000, the percentage of bachelor, master, and doctoral degree holders was about half of today's numbers. The labor market is becoming more and more competitive. It is more important than ever to update your skillset and document those skills through formal certifications and academic degrees. Having a continuous improvement or continuing

---

[87] (America Counts Staff, 2019)

education mindset will help you stay current and is an excellent leadership quality.

Nailing the Interview Process

One thing is for sure, you don't want to get to the face-to-face interview stage, go all the way through the selection process, and then blow your landing like Auburn's gymnast Samantha Cerio[88] and French gymnast Samir Aït Saïd[89]. If you haven't seen these epic falls, search YouTube, but beware, they contain graphic bone fractures.

BTW – Did you watch the videos? Did you feel a sense of horror? Have you got that sickening feeling in your stomach? Well, that's what it feels like to get to the last round of leadership interviews and epically fail. Make sure you're ready by preparing and rehearsing. However, if you do fail, get up, heal up, work it out, and try again, even if you need counseling.

When you start the interview process, expect to go through at least three to five interviews, and interview with multiple people. Leadership promotions are typically made either by committee or with significant feedback from the hiring manager's peers.

There are several things to consider in the interviewing process:

- Do your research on those who will interview you. Learn about them and get familiar with them as individuals and business people.

---

[88] (CelebrityTV, 2019)
[89] (KickMari Sports, 2016)

- Be prepared to give samples of your writing skills and to give a live presentation.
- Address your weaknesses. If you have never managed P & L before, what will you do in the first 90 days to address this shortcoming? If this is your first leadership role, review how you've prepared for the position and your action plan for improving your leadership skills while on the job.
- Have a 30, 60, and 90-day plan of action.
- It will take you six months to figure out what the heck you're doing in the role, and another six months to get good at it! Humility goes a long way. Don't be naive and try to "take command."
- Listen more than you talk. Show respect, and whatever you do, don't be a know-it-all.

Consider asking for a chance to demonstrate your ability to lead. Ask for the opportunity to present your portfolio of work and ideas that may be of value to the company. The top hires I have made were candidates able to demonstrate their abilities. It allowed me to dig deeper into who they were versus just listening to a typical superficial energetic style presentation. They were hands down the best interviewees, and it secured their roles on the leadership team.

There are excellent interviewing resources on the market. *"The First-Time Manager"* by Jim McCormick[90] is a useful resource that provides topic areas for which to prep for the interview process. The book also covers most of the duties of a first-time manager. Knowing them will help prepare you to answer interview questions intelligently.

---

[90] (McCormick, 2018)

Reflections

Take five minutes and reflect on what you've learned. Write down at least three takeaways. At the end of the book you will have 30+ key ideas to review that will help mold your thinking, build bridges, and bolster your leadership skills.

1._____

_____

_____

_____

_____

_____

2._____

_____

_____

_____

_____

_____

3._____

_____

_____

_____

_____

_____

_____

_____

_____

_____

_____

Chapter 6: Transformational Leadership

Looking Deeper than Single-Loop Leaders

A photographer was rummaging around in a box of old photographic glass negatives with scenes of Yosemite National Park. He thought they were cool because he used to work at the park, so he bought the box for $45. When he got them home, he took a closer look at them and realized that they might be the work of Ansel Adams. He took them to an expert who verified they were from Ansel Adams, and he sold them for $200 million. Yes, that's right, they were worth $200 million![91] The photographer looked past the surface and investigated the nature and characteristics of the negatives, which made him wealthy.

The garage sale owner was what we call a single-loop thinker. They look at the surface of things as they currently exist. The photographer was a double-loop thinker; a person who can see what's on the surface, but also digs deeper to find out what's behind or creating it. The single-loop thinker saw a $45 box of old photo negatives; the double-loop thinker saw a treasure worth $200 million.

It's Not Our Parents' Workplace Anymore

The Millennial workforce did not grow up in an analog, linear, "in-the-box" world, where knowledge was limited, choices were few, and societal standards were primarily uniform. Their assumptions, beliefs, and norms are as different as one kaleidoscope is from another. Each

---

[91] (Waldek, 2018)

generation, ethnicity, and culture around the globe has its own set of assumptions, beliefs, and norms as well. Effective leaders must dig deep into personal interactions and ask what are the underlying assumptions, ideas, and standards of today's workforce? Then to create motivated followers, they can match leadership strategies to the people, situation, and circumstances.

Leaders who are single-loop thinkers only look at surface levels and struggle to lead and motivate multi-generational and multi-cultural workforces. Likewise, for Millennials and Gen Z to become true leaders, you must also look deeper into the assumptions, beliefs, and norms of your Gen X and Baby Boomer predecessors and vice-versa.

Single-loop learners and thinkers assume that everyone had similar social experiences growing up and similar educational backgrounds. **Single-loopers manage their workforces as if everyone has the same assumptions, beliefs, and norms as they do.** However, in today's global society and information-based economy, the idea of uniformity is far from the reality in which we live and work. We all live in the same nation, yet our individual life experiences are different. We have shared and non-shared values. For those that are shared, we tend to rank them in differing orders. For those that are not shared, we must come to an understanding of those differences.

Single-loop (surface level) learning and thinking can influence leaders to choose authoritarian leadership styles that alienate their workers. **Workers feel devalued based on the hierarchy of authority and the division of labor and management.** It may also encourage reification. Reification is when an organization or leader views their employees as objects, no different than a desk or a pen. They treat each person in the workforce as if they were the same. **Single-loopers have a "one-size-fits-all" style of managing.** They view everyone as a static force, linear to their ideals, or at least they believe that everyone should think and behave as they do.[92]

For example, "Every manager has a mental model of the world in which he or she acts, based on their personal experiences and knowledge. When he or she thinks of behavior alternatives within their mental model, this is single-loop learning," Henry Mintzberg,[93] otherwise known as "thinking *inside* the box."

To visualize the concept, think of applying Henry Ford's manufacturing concepts of mass production to leading and managing an organization's human capital (the workforce). Single-loop leaders force people to think "inside the box," encouraging uniformity and making controlling business processes more manageable. However, single-loop thinking/leading crushes creativity, innovation, and individualism, which are vital to business growth.

Historical leadership models based on outdated assumptions, beliefs, and norms are becoming less effective, and their relevance will continue to diminish the more our workforce changes. It is time to say goodbye to ideals created in an analog, pre-technological workplace when agriculture and industrial manufacturing were the leading industries, and mainstream communication was by the pony express, telegraph, and snail-mail. Some leadership ideals have their underlying foundation back in the days of the

---

[92] (Bronner, 2011)
[93] (Cartwright, 2002)

Caesars, back to when the world was flat, and real horses were used for rating horsepower!

We Were Cogs in a Machine

Standardization was a central idea in birthing the great industrial revolution in America. It worked well up until the WWII era. Single-loop learning and thinking started showing its faults in the 1950s - 1970s. American manufacturing industries had developed a philosophy of producing as many products as possible without carefully considering defect rates. Consumers were at the mercy of whatever level of quality American corporations chose to build. Most cars died at around 100,000 miles, which meant consumers needed to buy a car every five to seven years. This was great for the manufacturers because it perpetuated the supply chain and product lifecycle until "Made in Japan" came along.

Management didn't care what the workers thought, either. They didn't listen to their ideas; they were just another gear in the great industrial machine. Management was top-down, command and control — those who suffered under this philosophy sponsored the birth of unions and collective bargaining.

With traditional single-loop thinking/leading in mind, I challenge you to watch Apple's 1984 Super Bowl commercial. At the time, it was revolutionary. Go to YouTube and search "Apple 1984 Commercial."[94]

The workers in the commercial are not from Russia or some oppressed Socialist/Communist nation; they were

---

94 (Apple, 1984)

Americans! The commercial was about freeing the American workforce from "single-loop" thinkers and leaders who exist only to serve themselves and the corporate machine.

We can no longer use single-loop thinking/leading. We cannot simply slap a "shiny coat of paint" or a "new set of tools and techniques" on top of an ineffective single-loop foundation. Industries and companies that began decades and even centuries ago are especially challenged to transform themselves into modern double and triple loop thinking and leading organizations. Deploying leadership and organization development strategies throughout a company can transverse this chasm.

Some shining examples of innovative, creative, and transformational leadership have come from the supply chain, manufacturing, and business services industries. Some of the world's most significant examples of success are companies such as Amazon, Whole Foods, Zappos, Unilever, and IBM. IBM is in the middle of a transformative leadership project using the FourSight Creative Thinking System, a methodology of creative problem solving for innovative thinking. IBM is bringing positive change to its traditional leadership thinking.[95]

Double-Loop Leaders Are Transformational

Effective leaders start at the double-loop learning/thinking level. Effective leaders can motivate not only their generation and culture but all the generations and cultures. How do double-loop thinkers lead?

---

[95] (FourSight, 2018)

Leaders who dig deeper into workplace interactions and understand that as time passes, society changes, and so must their foundational assumptions, beliefs, and norms from which they lead. They know that no two employees are alike, and therefore seek different ways to connect with and influence each individual. They value individualism and creativity.

The Millennial and Gen Z generations have grown up in the information age, an age of wonder, in a technology-based world, and their generations do not see the world the same as other generations. Their underlying assumptions, beliefs, values, and norms are different than their parents' and grandparents' generations, and that's ok, it is the ordinary course of societal growth.

If you are to gain followers, get promoted, and build healthy working relationships, you must understand how to work well under managers and manage those whose foundational assumptions, beliefs, values, and norms are different than yours. The same is true for our gender and culturally diverse workforce, as well. At a minimum, this requires you to be a double-loop thinker/leader.

Cultural and Emotional Intelligence

The good news is that new and emerging leadership strategies are proving to be highly successful at motivating our multi-generational, multi-cultural workforce. These strategies are improving productivity and effectiveness by encouraging and embracing creativity and innovation.

Two skills that can help get you promoted and create a sense of "yes we can" in a multi-generational, multi-cultural workforce are Cultural and Emotional Intelligence (CI and EI). Here are a couple of resources to guide you on developing these skills and abilities; for EI, Maureen Metcalf and Mark Palmer's, "*Innovative Leadership Fieldbook*" and David C. Thomas', "The Multi-Cultural Mind" for CI.

If you want to increase the probability of being promoted into leadership, you must gain a level of emotional and cultural intelligence beyond that of your peers. Becoming a double or even triple-loop thinker/leader will help transform you.

Embracing Creativity and Innovation

Double-loop thinkers are different. "Double-loop learning is an educational concept and process that involves teaching people to think more deeply about their assumptions and beliefs. It was created by Chris Argyris, a leading organizational trainer in the mid-1980s and developed over the next decade into an effective tool for transforming existing leadership and training new leaders".[96]

Double-loop thinkers/leaders embrace change. They question foundational ideals to make sure that they are still relevant for those they lead. They dig deep into their foundational assumptions, beliefs, and presumed norms, investigating their validity in the context of current socio-economical and socio-political environments. They use rational thinking to evaluate how to lead based on their specific set of circumstances in today's dynamic business environment.

Millennials and Gen Z embrace leadership models that stem from double and triple-loop thinking/leading. The foundation of their core values, workplace assumptions,

---

[96] (Cartwright, 2002)

beliefs, and norms span more than one culture. Today's leaders must understand this and begin to question the relevancy of their leadership ideas and methods. Once this is done, and a fresh set of leadership assumptions, beliefs, and norms are adopted, then and only then, can a leadership transformation take place. Change leadership requires a higher level of thinking. Organizations that adopt double-loop thinking will better their chances to keep pace with today's socio-economic and socio-political changes.

Triple-Loop Leaders are Strategic Visionaries

At the same time, America was pumping out large quantities of average lifespan cars, an American engineer and statistician, W. Edward Deming, had a creative, innovative idea. Through continuous process improvement, a company could produce as many products as possible while also reducing defects. Hence, they could mass-produce products at the highest quality level possible. **Triple-loop learning/thinking asks why systems and processes even exist.** Why do we believe what we believe? Why do we assume certain things, and why do we value what we do? It's at the heart of conceptual learning, strategic thinking, and visionary leadership.[97]   For example, in the 1950s, '60s, and '70s, American manufacturers assumed they were not at risk from global competition. Triple-loop thinking would have questioned their traditional paradigms and produced strategic thinkers and leaders. Is it possible that we could have avoided the loss of so many American manufacturing jobs if the leaders of that time would have been triple-loop thinkers? Maybe?!

---

[97] (Tosey, Visser, & Saunders, 2011)

Triple-loop thinking is at the heart of Total Quality Management (TQM), The Toyota Way, Six Sigma, Lean, and Lean Six Sigma. Today the Toyota Way is used around the world and has two main pillars, continuous process improvement and respect for people.[98] These processes added science to organizational leadership and transcended double-loop thinking to triple-loop thinking. Triple-loop learning and thinking is what America's greatest 20th century CEO, Jack Welch, used to transform General Electric (GE) and make it one of today's world-leading innovative corporations.

In a later chapter, we will dig deep into Mr. Welch's leadership career. He learned to lead over time, and his story is one of continuous improvement, learning, and leadership maturation. We will glean from the triumphs and the mishaps of his journey to greatness. Mr. Welch's leadership significantly influenced corporate Baby Boomer executives and organizational leadership training. To understand the way many Boomer and Gen X leaders think about leading, we need to study his career. Ignoring this icon of leadership and others like him, such as Lee Iacocca, would be foolish if we want to bridge the gap of understanding between generations. As a potential leader, you want to know what they taught about leading. We will dive deeper into some insights from Mr. Welch's career in the chapter on sources of leadership power.

---

[98] (Toyota, Inc., 2012)

Reflections

Take five minutes and reflect on what you've learned. Write down at least three takeaways. At the end of the book you will have 30+ key ideas to review that will help mold your thinking, build bridges, and bolster your leadership skills.

1._____

_____

_____

_____

_____

_____

2._____

_____

_____

_____

_____

_____

3._____

_____

_____

_____

_____

_____

_____

_____

_____

_____

Chapter 7: Leadership Power and Connections

Our bright young professionals need strong skills to lead our multi-generational and growingly multi-cultural workforce! This chapter is incredibly relevant for effective leadership because it discusses sources of power within corporations. It explains the behavioral effects they elicit, negative and positive, and how to lead effectively by using different sources of power.

I spent most of my career in an industry marked and sometimes marred by acquisitions and mergers. That business environment placed a significant burden on organizational leaders and managers to connect. Those who connected survived, and those who didn't connect left one way or another. It was in the middle of this acquisition and merger environment when I took my first national role. I had been recruited to help lead a change and revitalization initiative for a low-tech services company that had recently bought a division of a high-tech firm. The merger of the two had put a severe financial strain on the company. At the same time, new competition caused a loss in sales revenue, and the company was in the red. Their stock dropped to an all-time low as well.

I took the role because of the negative changes the "ice queen of the Northeast" brought to my former employer, and my new employer recruited me specifically on the CEO's promise of leading innovative change. The challenge of revitalizing the business was very attractive. So were the advancement opportunities success would bring. I reported directly to the Executive Vice President (EVP) and Senior Vice President (SVP), in charge of the initiative, and had an opportunity to connect with many of the organization's senior leaders. The change efforts went well, and I was able to connect with about half of the headquarters' (HQ) leaders and field management. The half I connected with came from the technology company and were double and triple-loop learners/thinkers. Triple-loop learners/thinkers go a step past double-loopers. They use the logical and creative parts of their brains to solve problems, strategize, and innovate. They are employees and leaders who can think logically as well as creatively, i.e., left-right thinkers. Double-loopers embrace change, triple-loopers are change agents who create, originate, and sponsor change.

The other half of the leaders who were from the lower-tech company were single-loop learners/thinkers and did not see the need for change. Fortunately for me, the high-tech company's leaders were running the show. We were able to steer the company in the right direction, and it became profitable again. My group and I set company and personal performance records. As the turn-around entered full velocity, the CEO announced he was retiring. When the single-loop thinkers/leaders heard he was retiring, they saw it as their opportunity to regain formal (legitimate) power over the company. Several of the board members had long-term relationships with many of the original single-loop leaders. Working together, they appointed a new CEO who came from the same low-tech background as the single-loop leaders. As a result, legitimate power shifted to the single-loop thinkers/leaders.

A few months later, the new CEO fired the EVP and shifted my boss's role to "SVP of Special Projects." "Special projects" is code for "we like you, but we're not sure what to do with you, and you should probably look for an opportunity outside the company." In two decisions, I lost a significant amount of my influence power. The company reorganized itself over the next six months dissolving our change management team. The new organization was more traditional and discouraged out-of-the-box (creative/innovative) thinking. I ended up taking a different national role and found myself reporting to a single-loop thinker/leader. Although I kept much of my legitimate power, over the next six months, my new SVP and those who gained legitimate power realized we had different leadership philosophies. At that point, I lost much of my referential power and began using expert power to keep my job. It was crystal clear that if I was going to ensure a lucrative employment situation and enjoy my work life, I needed to seek employment elsewhere and fast.

Fortunately, I had made lots of connections with our partners and ended up taking a higher role at a better company. There's an old saying, "if you help enough people get what they want, sooner or later, someone will help you get what you want," which is what happened. One of our partners for whom I had helped develop competitive advantages, and designed a go-to-market strategy to relaunch their software products, recommended me to one of his friends.

Informal and Formal Power

One of the first things to understand is that there are different types of leadership power. There is formal and informal leadership power, and you will need to master both to get promoted and to move into higher levels of leadership. There are also base sources of leadership power:

- Reward Power
- Coercive Power
- Legitimate Power
- Referent or Referential Power
- Expert Power
- Informational Power[99]

People within organizations also have power orientations such as being a high-power person or low-power person, competitive or cooperative power person. Finally, there are power dynamics within teams.[100] In this chapter, we will discuss the use and outcomes of several of the power bases. Regarding formal versus informal power, leaders with formal power/authority, must invite you to the leadership table and approve your promotion. Still, you will get that invitation by using informal and cooperative power such as referential power, rational persuasion, and personal appeal with those above you on the org chart. I cannot stress this enough from my own experience, research, and studying why leaders have come and gone.

Lessons from General Electric's Greatest CEO

As you seek and apply for leadership and executive roles, you will meet with and be evaluated by leaders who typically learned how to lead from "The *GE Way*"[101] and other strong leadership skills from the 1980s and 1990s. Pay attention and take notes in this section; it is incredibly important to understanding current leadership mindsets, using the various sources of leadership power effectively, and

---

[99] (Hughes & Ginnett, 2015)
[100] (Johnson & Johnson, 2013)
[101] (Slater, 1999)

avoiding the mistakes I and others have made early in our careers.

One of the notable corporate leaders we can study is Jack Welch of General Electric's (GE) fame. When he started his leadership journey, the business environment was in a season of transition. Through his leadership, GE was freed, from old manufacturing methodologies that were driving it into financial ruin, to embrace the operational philosophies of Total Quality Management (TQM) and Six Sigma. Along the way, he learned many leadership lessons. Understanding how to connect with all levels of leadership was needed to be an effective CEO. Without leadership coalitions, he would not be able to bring about the changes GE needed.

GE's Board of Directors initially rejected Mr. Welch as CEO. Can you imagine being the board members who refused the man who became the greatest CEO of the 1980s and '90s? No guru for you! LOL.

Coercive Power Produces Resentment

In the early years, Mr. Welch was devoted to technical knowledge and expertise. His work ethic reflected it in the fact that he worked long hours, weekends, and overshadowed his contemporaries regarding productivity and expertise. As a young manager, he:

- Used less effective sources of power, such as legitimate, coercive, and expert powers to enforce deadlines.
- Used pressure to try and influence his peers and subordinates into performing.

- Wanted to have the reputation for being driven to accomplish corporate goals.
- Desired to gain power and be promoted into higher levels of management, and he drove his business units hard.
- Was not a team builder, evidenced by his attitude that his co-workers were the competition.
- Wanted to be known as the person responsible for all project successes.[102]

Mr. Welch's followers reacted to his original leadership style with compliance. They feared punishment and complied with his requests accordingly. Mr. Welch did not use reward as a power source, and this displayed his attitude of self-promotion, which humiliated and demoralized those that worked under him. Mr. Welch's constant pressure to perform resulted in his staff's extreme stress. His leadership put a strain on their work-life balance, lowering their quality of life.

At the time of his first major promotion, one of his peers who also sought promotion, tried to derail his career. Mr. Welch's peer was so angered by his unmistakable drive to succeed; he filed false reports about him. Mr. Welch always had a low tolerance for ambiguity; he hated dogmatism and maintained an active internal locus of control. He always believed he was in control of his destiny. After the attempted derailing, Mr. Welch asked himself, why did his co-worker react that way to his leadership? He realized that the very trait he hated in his co-worker, self-promotion at any cost, was expressed in his attitude as a leader. He relished in the

---

[102] (Slater, 1999)

idea of promotion over his rivals, and his peers knew it. Mr. Welch's personal life began to suffer, as well.[103]

He was promoted to a vice president because of his business unit's productivity; however, he had never learned how to use referential power or other influencing strategies. His relationships with his new peers and subordinates also became strained. As he reflected on his lack of success, he realized he needed to change his strategies.

As vice president, his direct reports continued to comply with his orders. They gave no extra effort beyond what was required. However, Mr. Welch was able to convince the plant managers that he had the company's and workers' best interests in mind and that his changes, including layoffs, would eventually allow as many people as possible to retain their jobs. He earned a reputation of having intolerance for low performance, and his downsizing of staff caused reactions of fear and leadership resistance. His ability to lead other leaders became diminished.

Influence Power Creates Commitment

As time went on, Mr. Welch, began to express more empathy toward the line workers and his staff, and he began to:

- Connect with others in the company.
- Socialize with other leaders, including the union bosses.
- Develop relationships with other leaders and employees, allowing him to begin to use coalitions.

---

[103] (Slater, 1999)

- Hold consultations with other managers and leaders.
- Form coalitions with line workers to successfully motivate union leaders in negotiation for the contracts needed to implement profitable changes.

He was learning to build relationships that opened referential power, rational persuasion, and personal appeal to get people to commit to his ideas. Although his values hadn't changed much, his strategies did. He was able to accomplish the tasks given to him, and his focus turned to develop new leadership skills.[104]

As a result of the changes he made, he was promoted first to senior vice president, then chairman and CEO. His focus was no longer on managing processes. His belief that leadership must be visionary and guide the corporation was his focus, and it affected his behavioral choices. He began to use better sources of power:

- Reward
- Reference
- Rational Persuasion
- Inspiration
- Personal Appeal

It took almost two years of persistence with union leaders before he began to gain the referential power he needed. By using coalitions, consultations, and exchange, he won them over. He created bonuses for production line managers, secured positions for union leaders, and encouraged better performance by rewarding the reduction of product defects.

---

[104] (Slater, 1999)

Mr. Welch's trend in getting subordinates and even other senior leaders to commit to his vision for GE continued through the rest of his career.[105]

The ABC's of Ranking Leadership

As Mr. Welch progressed as a leader, he learned the importance of introspection. While looking at himself, and his attitudes and actions, he realized he was self-centered. He then identified and tried to deal with the reasons why. As he realized the maturing power of introspection, he also began analyzing the successes and failures of GE and its leaders. He began to look for ways to repeat strengths and weed out weaknesses. Mr. Welch hated bureaucracy. He felt that companies should have a small business feel and that leaders should be able to easily change what they felt was holding the company back from profitability. His belief in corporate nimbleness and his commitment to observation, reflection, evaluation, and change led him to implement the Six Sigma methodology at GE.

When he took over GE, there was a lack of a centralized theory of leadership and management. The local plant managers did as they saw fit leading to a disconnect between operational and planning functions within the organization. To bring centralized leadership to the company, he created levels of leadership, placing managers into A, B, and C-list groups. He used reward power to inspire them to improve to the next level. The A, B, C model created an in-group, a middle-group, and an out-group. For those in the A group, the future was bright. B-listers were encouraged to improve and want to be an A player. C-listers knew they were not promotable. Some B-listers and many C-players became

---

[105] (Slater, 1999)

demoralized and left GE. They sought companies where they would have better upward mobility in management.

One example was the practice of firing the bottom 10% of managers each year, which Mr. Welch felt was the right amount of pressure to motivate the staff to perform. This practice cost him the chairman of the board of directors position for many years. It was not until there was a change in the board of directors that he was able to become chairman of the board.[106] Using Six Sigma also came into question. It is an exceptional process to rescue struggling manufacturing operations; however, it chokes the creativity out of regular employees and middle management who are the life source of every organization. As GE's state changed from being a struggling manufacturer to a high-growth global leader, the use of Six Sigma added layers of bureaucracy. Ironically, the process that helped GE began to choke out the innovative thinking that had saved it.

Mr. Welch should have worked to understand the differences in people's motivations. His A, B, C-list leadership program did not take into consideration that people are motivated differently. It should have allowed for differences in personal values as well. Had he added these types of attributes, the A, B, C-list may have worked long term. Business units need the flexibility to adapt programs to their local culture. Corporate cultures must adapt according to local, regional, and national business, political, and ethnic cultural influences. Emotional and Cultural Intelligence, as well as Appreciative Inquiry methodologies, could have helped GE avoid losses in lower levels of leadership.

---

[106] (Welch & & Byrne, 2009)

Today's generation of leaders must find ways to make workers feel appreciated and valued. Mr. Welch's A, B, C leadership team approach worked at first but encouraged so much internal competition that C group members just left the company leaving a gap in lower and middle management. As our culture continues to shift toward the values of equality, diversity, and personal affirmation, using material rewards as a motivation tool will continue to lose effectiveness. High caliber people, especially Millennials and Gen Z, will not put up with managers that pressure them without valuing them, or treat them as a cog in a machine, or do not respect them as a person and their personal life. Weaving in new methodologies into current leadership training and development programs will help transform. **Positive psychology methods, emotional intelligence, cultural intelligence, and appreciative inquiry will be some of the foundation stones for next-gen leadership programs.**

Traits to Replicate

Few others have had such a strong work ethic or the vision to build a leadership development program to produce global executives at an unprecedented rate as Mr. Welch's program. It increased communication, centralized leadership, strengthened leadership coalitions, and streamlined management processes. Mr. Welch's ability to adapt through observation, reflection, and change was his single biggest asset throughout his career. It allowed him to separate failures and turn them into opportunities for improvement.

Mr. Welch understood that leadership, not management, was the way of the future, that companies must develop their leaders. As the Gen X and Millennial generations take the reins, leadership development and training is more important now than ever and as Gen Z comes aboard, the need will intensify.

If we are to follow his sound traits, it was his ability to change that was the secret to his success. In every situation, he records that he had to change the strategies he used, many times, inventing them according to what the case required. **We must do the same as Gen X, and Millennial generations take the corporate reigns, and Gen Z leaders begin to emerge.**

Traits to Avoid

Although he was able to learn and change his leadership strategies, this leader's biggest failure was his inability to change his value system and base behavioral traits. Values and characteristics (personal attributes) such as emotional and cultural intelligence and work-life balance values are hard to improve on your own. When he began to see the effects of his negative behaviors, he should have sought help to find and address the root causes. Instead, he superficially changed practices to fit the moment to get what he wanted. Later these underlying faults caused undue stress in his life due to cognitive dissonance, which was very apparent when dealing with European leaders. He didn't change his style or consider situations based on different cultures and ethnicity. **A truly successful leader must be able to cross the aisle and have a relationship with other cultures and differing ethnicities.**

With the gross failure of so many well-known figures lately, is it any wonder that Millennial and Gen Z generations may shy away from certain types of leaders or reject the ways earlier generations have led? They do not want a life of high stress, divorce, failed parenthood, and emotional pain, to say they are a vice president or drive a Lexus. Millennials are the first generation to stand up and say no to post World War II materialistic values. Gen Z feels even stronger about their personal lives.

Leadership is both an art and a science. Leaders are not born; they are developed. We must create or recreate current leadership programs to help organizations recognize leadership potential in a way that promotes a positive work environment free from internal competition.[107] Had Mr. Welch polled his leaders to check for morale and loyalty, he may have observed his problems early enough to correct them. Instead, as his success grew, he isolated himself from lower-level organizational input. He stopped applying his observation, reflection, and personal continuous improvement mindset, ultimately costing him in the end.[108]

Lessons Learned

Leaders and followers should take inventory assessments of their values, traits, emotional intelligence, knowledge, and skills. Make sure to hire people that are different than you. Guiding and leading a corporation requires different skillsets and ways of thinking. Not everyone thinks like a traditional American. Getting input from international people and different ethnic groups is essential to succeed in a global economy.

Focus on using referential, reward, rational persuasion, and personal appeal power when possible. These help people gain respect for you as a leader and create an atmosphere where people want to follow you. Use your charisma

---

[107] (Hughes & Ginnett, 2015)
[108] (Welch & & Byrne, 2009)

carefully and not for personal gain at the cost of others. When trying to influence and motivate others, find out what is meaningful to them first. Think about what we discussed in the previous chapters. Can you see how referential and reward power are compatible with transformational leadership? **Can you see how Mr. Welch grew from coercing followers to cultivating passionate voluntary followers?** When you need to motivate your team, think about which way the source of authority and power you are going to use leans. Does it lean toward pressure and coercion or positive psychology and motivation? Then, choose wisely.

We should apply observation, reflection, continuous improvement, and change management, as Mr. Welch did. These were common threads throughout his successes (and failures when he did not employ them). These practices will assist the current and upcoming generations of leaders to keep open minds. They will need to embrace innovative leadership styles and adapt their strategies to the ever-changing and shifting VUCA world in which we live and work.

Reflections

Take five minutes and reflect on what you've learned. Write down at least three takeaways. At the end of the book you will have 30+ key ideas to review that will help mold your thinking, build bridges, and bolster your leadership skills.

1._____

_____

_____

_____

_____

2._____

_____

_____

_____

_____

3._____

_____

_____

_____

_____

_____

_____

_____

Chapter 8: Servant-Based Leadership

What is Servant-Based Leadership?

This past year I have talked with a couple of hundred people from all generations. When I ask Traditionalists and Baby Boomers about servant-based leadership, most of them scoff. When I ask Gen X about it, they say they've heard about it, think for the most part it has good qualities, and wish that their bosses afforded them the personal appreciation that comes along with it.

When I ask Millennials and Gen Z, the first thing they do is ask what it is. I explain it this way, it's a method of leadership, where leaders appreciate the efforts of those who work for them and see their leadership role as one that mentors and equips their followers for success. The company provides the tools, training, coaching, and creates a positive business environment resulting in employee satisfaction and gratitude. In helping their staff succeed, they ensure their success. This positive work environment enhances team cohesion and promotes genuine communication and care for one another as individuals.[109] Millennials and Gen Z's overwhelming response was, "What other kinds of leadership are there?!"

Scholarly researchers have found that Millennials perform better as individuals and in workgroups when led by servant-based leadership.[110] Servant-based leadership cultivates followers who want to follow the leader. I recommend all leaders incorporate servant leadership methods into their skillset. This chapter explores aspects of servant leadership.

---

[109] (Center for Servant Based Leadership, 2016).
[110] (VanMeter, Grisaffe, Chonko, & Roberts, 2013)

Robert K. Greenleaf developed Servant Leadership into a formal theory in the 1970s. Its ideas, however, date back 2000 years. Its principles are the opposite of leader-focused leadership. Older generations primarily learned leader-focused methodologies, which places importance on the leader while showing little appreciation and reward for their subordinates (followers). They are used to subordinates following not from an atmosphere of reciprocal appreciation, but one of coercion, authoritarian rule, and transactional employment arrangements. However, all people want to feel appreciated and rewarded for their work.[111] Skip Prichard, another servant-based leadership developer, lists the top nine qualities of a servant-based leader:

- Values diverse opinions.
- Cultivates a culture of trust.
- Develops other leaders.
- Helps people with life issues.
- Encourages others.
- Sells (shares and cares) instead of tells.
- Thinks you, not me.
- Thinks long term.
- Acts with humility.[112]

Rocking the Kasbah of Authoritarian Leadership

What's a Kasbah? Think of a movie filmed in Africa or the Middle East. A Kasbah is a fortress or inner set of buildings in each city that protected the people from attack. Some of

---

[111] (Center for Servant Based Leadership, 2016)
[112] (Prichard, 2013)

them have stood for hundreds and thousands of years. Kasbahs are from a time when there was very little social change, low technology, when the economy was agrarian, kings, sultans, and pharaohs ruled, and religion and social customs governed human thought as opposed to science and reason. In those days the leaders maintained the status quo and spread their own likeness, traditions, and greatness in grandiose conquests and projects. They judged themselves by what happened in and to the Kasbah of their cities where their traditions were passed on as a legacy to their descendants and as a monument to themselves. The leadership of those days can be judged by history. What happened to the Kasbah in their city? As time passed and knowledge increased, Kasbahs either flourished by embracing change or were abandoned and reclaimed by the desert.

In many parts of the world, leadership and management ideals changed very little over thousands of years. Some of the earliest leadership philosophies or ways of thinking about governing and leading, date all the way back to ancient Greece when Aristotle wrote his *"Nicomachean Ethics"* and *"Politics"* collections. At that time, personal characteristics and preferences began to be discussed as leadership qualities and many of the ancient Greek philosophers' ideals are still used in management theories today.[113]

The Greeks were masters of politics and rocked the Kasbah of historic society. Their leadership philosophies and theories had strong followings and were used to govern thriving poleis (cities) and nations. Plato's challenge of the

---

[113] (Ross, 2009)

status quo cost him his life as described by Socrates in "The Republic".[114] These Greek philosophers were the first in the western world to contemplate importance of personal centers of locus such as Idealism and Relativism. Idealists believe in a stated and stable group of rights and wrongs, whereas Relativists define what is right and wrong based upon current circumstances, situations, and environments.

Forsyth's, "*A Taxonomy of Ethical Ideologies*"[115], defines four ethical orientations:

- Situationists, which score high in relativism and idealism.
- Absolutists, which are high on idealism and low on relativism.
- Subjectivists, which score high on relativism and low on idealism.
- Exceptionists, which are low on both.[116]

What 'rocks the Kasbah' of today's workplace orientation, is that no matter what category Millennials fall into, they are more likely to be forgiving and overlook ethical violations than other generations. Absolutists judge violations most severely and subjectivists are the most lenient. This propensity to forgive their peers' ethical violations and give them additional chances to succeed deepens the Millennial generation's embracement of transformational, servant-based, and socially conscious leadership methods.

---

[114] (Morgan, 2006)
[115] (Forsyth, 1980)
[116] (Forsyth, 1980)

Another fascinating truth about the younger generations is that when led by servant-based leadership models, they perform better. Whether their ethical beliefs lean toward idealism or relativism, they perform better as individuals and in workgroups and have fewer ethical workplace violations.[117] They are more socially aware than their older counterparts. Some Millennials have even stated that they place their followers' and direct reports' wellbeing above that of the organizations for which they work.

The socially conscious, positive aspects of servant-based leadership connect with younger generations who are more socially communal and collaborative in group orientations. Research shows that the stronger the degree of servant leadership, the stronger the working relationships produced, thereby lowering the tolerance of collaborative, ethical violations.[118] The bottom line is, younger generations are more productive, happy, ethical, and work better when led by a servant-based leadership model.

The Golden Rule

A leader's followers must follow voluntarily, not by force or coercion. In our modern, fast-paced society, it seems that we sometimes forget that we must be willing to learn how to be a leader before we can fill a leadership position. It is also interesting that when asked to lead, many people are unwilling, but when asked to help, they are willing to follow and do much of the work. There may be many reasons for this phenomenon. As it relates to leadership, the single most considerable step toward becoming a leader might be the

---

[117] (VanMeter, Grisaffe, Chonko, & Roberts, 2013)
[118] (VanMeter, Grisaffe, Chonko, & Roberts, 2013)

willingness to say, "I will learn to lead," and then ask people to follow voluntarily.

Once a person has committed to learning how to lead, they must ask, "what do I do now?" In servant leadership, a guiding principle behind "what should I do?" is the well-known golden rule. That is, a leader should weigh all actions and decisions from the perspective of 'do unto others as you would want to be done to you.' Even without further knowledge of leadership principles, following the golden rule will be a reliable guide to a leader's path.[119]

Learning to gain voluntary followers and using the golden rule are two of a strong leader's guidelines. Now, what to do to get started? Start thinking from a follower's perspective. Everyone is a follower. Even leaders follow other leaders. The best view of what a leader should do can be seen through the eyes of a follower. Ask yourself, what makes you want to follow someone voluntarily?

A leader must have followers. If there is an opportunity to lead, the presumption is that there is a group of followers needing a leader, e.g., a work department, a project team, a volunteer group, a family, etc. If the people that you are trying to rally to complete a task or goal are not willfully following you, you are not a leader (or at least not a good one). Leaders inspire people to want to work towards a set of goals, and that want, that desire, needs to transcend the benefits they will personally gain. Some would refer to this as working for the greater good, the good of the team, or the organization.

---

[119] (Buschman, 2017)

It is important to note that most good leaders are also good followers. Learning how to be a good follower is a skill. As a follower, quiz yourself:

- If I were the leader, how would I rate myself as a follower?
- What kind of followers would I want?
- How would I want them to interact internally with peers and externally with clients and partners?
- Why would anyone want to follow me willingly?
- What would motivate them to work and give an effort that goes beyond what is required?

Write these qualities down and use them as a guide to help you develop as a leader. Use them to help coach and develop your followers, and to search out training for leadership skill development.

Reflections

Take five minutes and reflect on what you've learned. Write down at least three takeaways. At the end of the book you will have 30+ key ideas to review that will help mold your thinking, build bridges, and bolster your leadership skills.

1._____

_____

_____

_____

_____

_____

2._____

_____

_____

_____

_____

_____

3._____

_____

_____

_____

_____

_____

_____

_____

_____

_____

_____

_____

Chapter 9: Unlocking Team Power

A Steaming Cup of Komodo Dragon

Over a steaming cup of Komodo Dragon with whole milk, three Splendas, and a dusting of nutmeg and cinnamon, a friend of mine told me about her rise to senior leadership. Years earlier, she had taken over a workgroup made up of tenured employees who were all older than she. The average seniority of the group was 25 years. Her role was to help them engage current and new customers to buy a new scan-and-pay technology her company had developed. The team was known for chewing up and spitting out new managers, and she had to overcome the team's years of negativity. The group was disengaged, below performance goals, and rumors were some of them worked side jobs while pretending to be at client sites!

She could have gone in and "ripped them a new one" like others had in the past and failed and continued the corporate insanity. BTW - Have you ever experienced this? Senior management hires the same type of person repeatedly, and the new hires fail every time. Yet management can't figure out why the company isn't growing?! Sorry, I got sidetracked thinking about leadership insanity...back to the story. Instead, my friend chose a different, creative route.

To reinvigorate the team, she focused on their strengths and didn't tell them how bad they were. She also didn't give them performance reviews to document why she should fire them, or to put them on a performance plan. NO! She focused on strengths, gained their trust, and won their hearts and minds. The same lagging team went on to work for her with passion and dedication, and she became a senior enterprise account manager.

Note to All: If you haven't been through training on emotional intelligence or cultural intelligence, do so. They are critical success factors for today's leaders. They are foundational for understanding how to coach and lead employees in our complex, modern workplace.

Appreciative Inquiry (AI)

Appreciative Inquiry's (AI) roots are in positive psychology. AI is a practice that requires Emotional Intelligence (EI) or Cultural Intelligence (CI). **By exercising AI principles, and using in EI and CI skills, leaders can unlock their team's power.** Six key factors in unlocking the potential of your existing staff and emerging leaders revolve around freedom. America's culture of freedom is what made our economy the greatest on earth. Liberating the latent power that already exists in our current workforce costs little but may win the future. In the *"Change Handbook,"* Cooperrider and Whitney list the six freedom factors for Appreciative Inquiry, (AI) as:

- The freedom to be known in respected work relationships.
- The freedom to be heard.
- The freedom to dream in community.
- The freedom to choose to contribute.
- The freedom to act with support.
- The freedom to be positive.[120]

---

[120] (Brown, Homer, & Isaacs, 2007)

AI helps free up and use the latent knowledge bottled up in your current staff. Free up your staff by weeding out the negative, build on your strengths, and transform your workplace.

Alan Webber, of the Harvard Business Review, said, "In the new economy, conversations are the most important form of work." Advanced problem-solving and growth communication methods using AI, help locate the status and health of your organization and its staff.[121] Two of these methods are Future Search and World Café. Future Search is a technique that assists leaders in creating change strategies for a brighter, more successful future. World Café meetings bring employees from all organizational levels together to brainstorm, solve problems, tear down barriers, and build bridges to implement change and growth strategies. AI takes full advantage of your existing workforce's talents, ideas, and intellect. A few of the companies who have reaped AI's benefits are; Verizon, the FAA, IKEA, City of Denver, Hunter Douglas, British Airways, and many more.

A great tragedy in traditional business communication is that many organizations still employ top-down, command and control. "I say, you do," management assumes those higher on the org chart have all the answers or to posture as if they do. Command and control creates an atmosphere that views or makes subordinates feel inferior to their managers, hides new talent, is afraid of others' high performance, and breaks almost every rule of sound leadership I've studied. BTW - Millennials hate it.

---

[121] (Brown, Homer, & Isaacs, 2007)

Please consider holding a series of AI events to assess the health of your company. **Listen to those who are on the front line, in the trenches, and working in mid-management.** Find out how employees feel about your organization's structure and leadership practices, and whether they are unleashing team power or stunting your organization's growth.[122]

Mentoring and Reverse Mentoring

The Bureau of Labor Statistics projects, "between 2014 and 2024, 36.4 million workers will enter the labor force, and 28.6 million will leave".[123] Its statistics reveal that the makeup of the workforce is changing; it is getting older.[124] Considering the changes coming and the effects they will have on team power, leaders need to re-evaluate their current workgroup makeup. If the team mix doesn't represent members from all stages of life and different skillsets, change it. Start thinking about pairing emerging leaders with retiring leaders so that there is at least one leader in the bullpen. Encourage retirees to mentor incoming leaders. Leaders must begin looking at upcoming retirements and promotions and purposefully create transition plans. There are so many Boomers who will retire; it is crucial to help prevent the loss of institutional knowledge and wisdom.

Those in leadership should be able to lead and manage the diverse workforce and adapt to these inevitable changes. Current and emerging leaders need to embrace their

---

[122] (The World Cafe, 2019)
[123] (U.S. Bureau of Labor Statistics, 2015)
[124] (U.S. Bureau of Labor Statistics, 2019)

generational differences to avoid significant talent and performance deficits as this transition takes place.[125]

When it comes to change, it's a good idea to be an early adopter and not a laggard. It's not enough to go with the current flow. Leaders must be able to identify future needs. Over the next ten years, in the public and private sectors, leadership training and mentoring programs will be crucial. Management should consider using mentorship programs, generational diversity training, and enhanced communication methods. These can reach and accommodate each generation's preferences fostering productivity that supports the work environment.[126] Not taking advantage of the wisdom and knowledge of those who will be retiring makes no sense. Mentoring younger leaders infuses purpose and meaning into the latter days of a person's career and helps re-engage disengaged workers.

Millennials and Gen Z, take note! Someone once said, if all your friends are in low places, then low places are where you'll end up. If you don't have any friends up the leadership chain, who can help you get into or move up in leadership? As Millennials and Gen Z, your generations embrace technology and are comfortable with change.[127] A way to learn leadership skills, help your company reinvigorate disengaged workers, and build a relationship with those in higher places, is to use technology to engage in reverse mentoring. Millennials and Gen Z can develop leadership skills and enhance job skills by using technology to mentor and train the older generations on technology skills.[128] You

---

[125] (Green & Roberts, 2012)
[126] (Kapoor & Solomon, 2011)
[127] (Kapoor & Solomon, 2011)
[128] (Green & Roberts, 2012)

already use technology as a resource for entertainment and problem-solving. Use your technology prowess as an advantage to assist those who are less tech-savvy.

Millennials and Team Power

Millennials are not a disconnected group of people that only have their sights set on fulfilling their own needs. They are passionate, adventurous, and sympathetic individuals who have Boomers and Gen Xers as major influencers and role models. Parents of Millennials used nurturing methods in their upbringing and led by example. Hinote and Sundvall, two researchers, believe that the strengths of Millennials outweigh their weaknesses, and as leaders, we must harness their creative power, enthusiasm, and ability to work in teams.[129] Kouzes and Posner, authors of *"The Leadership Challenge,"* explained that when leaders lead by example, the employees see their commitment.[130] Jarrett Spiro, assistant professor of organizational behavior at INSEAD, found "that while money is important to Millennials, their key motivator is maintaining a work-life balance, seeking out companies that foster strong workplace relationships, promote a sense of purpose, or make a difference."[131]

The Millennial and Gen Z generations are waiting for the opportunity to prove their abilities. They have the perfect mix of team skills. Team power is a vital component of navigating our VUCA world successfully. No matter what we do or who we are, we work, learn, play, and live in teams. We experience life together, whether as a family, group of friends, co-workers, or leadership team. Team

---

[129] (Hinote & Sundvall, 2015)
[130] (Kouzes & Posner, 2017)
[131] (Kapoor & Solomon, 2011)

development and group dynamics strategies are people-centered and dramatically affect organizational performance and improve decision making. It promotes democratic, participative management methods. High-performance teams have learned to unlock team power.

One of the best resources to understand group dynamics and how to unlock team power is *"Joining Together: Group Theory and Group Skills,"* by Johnson and Johnson. In their book, they apply many concepts to managing groups and the interpersonal interactions which occur. The topics they cover are:

- Group Formation.
- Group Goals, Social Interdependence, and Trust.
- Group Communication.
- Leadership within Groups.
- The Use and Sources of Power within Groups.
- The Processes of Decision-making.
- Handling Controversy and Fostering Creativity.
- Managing Conflicts of Interest.
- Diversity within Groups.[132]

Decision making is proven to be more successful when done by group consensus. Wise leaders gather information from their team and engage them to answer mission-critical questions. Johnson and Johnson share strategies for decision-making and incorporating creative problem-solving (CPS). Creative problem-solving has its roots in team dynamics. **There is no getting away from the need to learn how to motivate, facilitate, and lead teams.** I recommend that if you choose no other book to read, make it Johnson and

---

[132] (Johnson & Johnson, 2013)

Johnson's![133] I guarantee not only will you become a better follower and teammate, but you will also recognize those in your organization who have strong leadership skills and those who don't.

Consider this; unless you are leading a group of one, no matter what you do or where you go, you will need to understand how to be a good teammate and a good team leader. Even as a senior manager, you must interact with your peers. Leadership cooperation depends upon understanding how to make goals interdependent between teams and divisions.

Interdependence and Collaboration

A critical success factor in building an agile, market-responsive organization is interdependence. In the section on change-resistant leaders, I touched on organizational agreement. When company leaders agree with the corporate vision and cooperate with each other, its divisions are empowered to work together toward a set of common goals. To facilitate cooperation, organizations need strong mission and vision statements, visionary leadership, and collaborative corporate culture.[134]

Positive interdependence happens when leadership purposefully designs goals so that they are only achievable if other team members, departments, and divisions meet their goals. When an organization's design includes positive interdependence, lateral communications open, and barriers caused by the silo effect diminish.[135] **Organization**

---

[133] (Johnson & Johnson, 2013)
[134] (Inamori, 2013)
[135] (Galbraith, Downey, & Kates, 2001)

design/redesign must incorporate the ideas of interdependence, collaboration, lateral communication, and cooperation to unlock team power.

One U.S. multi-national corporation (MNC) I've interacted with, reorganized itself five times in ten years, from 2009 to 2019. What's incredible is that except for one reorg, the company's performance did not improve. As a matter of fact, in half of its divisions, the company's performance suffered. The company was trying to become an industry leader and adopt innovative ways to drive revenue; however, it had negative interdependence.

Negative interdependence happens when reward systems and goals are contradictory or in competition with one another. Success in one area of the company comes at the expense of another part of the business. In this case, the performance measurements and compensation plans rewarded contradicting behaviors. If one division was successful, it came at the expense of another division. If one manager earned a bonus, another manager suffered, sometimes in the same office! Even the sales compensation plans were opposed to each other. Competing goals create dysfunctional internal competition and silos. Their reward systems are set up to produce negative interdependence. Each time one division improved performance, another division lagged.[136] An organization divided against itself will not succeed. Each time this company reorganized, it was due to one set of leaders trying to gain control over a competing division that was causing it to suffer. Once a new set of leaders took control, they fired or used a reduction in force (RIF) to get rid of the high performers who caused them the

---

[136] (Johnson & Johnson, 2013)

most discomfort. In one of their moves, they gutted their change management team and technical support staff, the very leaders and workgroups who were driving change and the most profitable part of the business. It is no wonder why their most recent reorganization and RIF was due to lack of performance.

Neutral interdependence also exists. Many organizations create open lines of communication and encourage interaction and collaboration, which is the right thing to do. **However, interaction and collaboration are different from interdependence.** Goal interdependence builds a dynamic that places a portion of each team member's and division's success in the hands of their teammates and leadership peers. **To unlock team power, find ways to create goals that create cooperative, collaborative, and interdependent team environments.** Make decisions by consensus to help ensure they harmonize with the organizational mission and vision. Although consensus takes longer, it is proven to produce the most correct and best decisions. Consensus also encourages creativity, diversity, and open communication.

Know Your Why and Set Clear Goals

Once you are committed to unleashing your team's power, the first thing the team needs to know is, where are they going, why, and how are they going to get there? The first step for you as the leader is to define a set of interdependent goals and objectives. Many teams create a team charter that communicates the purpose, goals, and dynamics of how the team will function. I highly encourage this practice. **It's best to describe the idea of interdependence during the team formation process.** Interdependence might be a new and possibly strange concept to some of the team members. Make sure each member agrees with and understands this concept and how others, such as group decision-making, role assignments, and conflict resolution, will be handled.

Most followers are highly motivated if they know the why behind what they are doing. Take the time to write clear and concise mission and vision statements for the team. **Creating a team motto is a great idea as well and helps create a feeling of team unity.** I have used two team mottoes for years. The first is, "Nothing great happens without teamwork." The second is, "No one of us is as smart as all of us." I coined these phrases after reading, "*The Seventeen Indisputable Laws of Teamwork*" by John Maxwell.[137] If there is a clear set of interdependent goals, then a measurement system can be established and used to measure progress during project execution. It will also rate the quality of work, success, or failure at the end of the project. Also, a communication system must be in place. There are many communication models. Open communication is the most effective. There are also a variety of communication tools from which to choose, i.e., periodic review meetings, collaboration software, email, group IM (text) apps, etc.

During project execution, team members need to know who to look to as the leader of each task. Ensure that adequate resources are available to do the work. The measurement and communication systems will provide insight into conditions where resources are lacking.

All the above now become elements of the documented project outline. One pitfall for a leader is to presume that he is the one to build a complete and final plan. The reality is that the best project plans are ones developed by the entire

---

[137] (Maxwell, 2013)

team after discussing goals and objectives. There should be full buy-in by all team members. If the buy-in is not universal, do not proceed until it is. The plan does not need to have all the infinite details at the start. Add amendments along the way as necessary, and flesh out details as they arise and are understood. At the end of the project, the project plan will serve as a good source of documentation of the goals accomplished, the team effort, degree of success, etc.

Team members also want the freedom to do their work. A leader should avoid micromanagement. Team leadership facilitates teamwork. It doesn't dictate it. Dictating and micromanagement rob team members of their creativity and build barriers to applying individual skills and talents. Micromanagement bottles up team power, facilitating teamwork unlocks it.[138]

Celebrating Team Success

Followers desire feedback on their work and recognition for success as steps in the plan are completed. Most often, this is not money, although, at times, bonuses are appropriate. However, a leader must be even-handed when recognizing team members. Unequal treatment is a substantial disincentive and will destroy a team's effort. Set milestones, and when the workgroup reaches them, celebrate. At the successful completion of a project, celebrate again! A good leader needs to cheer the team forward. Theresa Amabile of Harvard Business School is one of the world's expert resources for driving team participation and morale. Her book, "*The Progress Principle*," will guide you in applying positive psychology and using reward power in teams.[139]

---

[138] (Johnson & Johnson, 2013)
[139] (Amabile & Kramer, 2011)

Does following the above principles guarantee success? No. Life has a way of "pitching" leaders high and tight, followed by sliders and curveballs. However, by following your plan and these guidelines, you will maximize the opportunity for success. Leaders are adaptable, flexible, forgiving, and realistic. Be positive and give the best you have to offer and follow your plan![140]

---

[140] (Buschman, 2017)

Reflections

Take five minutes and reflect on what you've learned. Write down at least three takeaways. At the end of the book you will have 30+ key ideas to review that will help mold your thinking, build bridges, and bolster your leadership skills.

1._____

_____

_____

_____

_____

_____

2._____

_____

_____

_____

_____

3._____

_____

_____

_____

_____

_____

_____

_____

_____

_____

Chapter 10: Leadership for Growth

In Chapter 1, I mentioned the five pillars of organization leadership for growth:

- Challenging the status quo with positive innovation.
- Inspiring a vision and set of goals that result in mutual commitment from all employees.
- Building teams that are empowered and are interdependent upon one other to succeed.
- Modeling the behaviors you espouse to others.
- Encouraging the hearts of employees so that they work through difficult times, striving to achieve the mutual vision and goals set before them.[141]

Throughout the book, I have touched on each of these areas. I hope that you are enjoying the journey and have gleaned useful tips on the art and science of leadership.

As the world's best leaders develop strategies and business models to ensure growth in the VUCA world, leadership itself is evolving. Leaders are designing organizations strategically to create autopoietic systems (auto-poy-etic systems: life-sustaining systems that reproduce and perpetuate themselves automatically).[142] When designed well, they cut waste and weed out unhealthy processes. Creating and maintaining autopoietic systems keeps organizations vital, full of life, and promotes growth and the revitalization of stalled initiatives.[143] In this chapter, we will

---

[141] (Johnson & Johnson, 2013)
[142] (Seidi, 2004)
[143] (Morgan, 2006)

explore four strategic tools that encourage autopoietic system creation.

The four strategic tools are:

- System Thinking
- Positive People Management
- Creative Problem Solving
- Continuous Process Improvement

These tools unlock leadership and workforce creativity and innovation. The global supply chain is looking for higher-level leaders who understand these strategies.[144]

System Thinking

Let's revisit my first national role. My task was to help lead a corporate cultural change, which would result in revitalizing the company. Before joining the company, its history was one of fast growth and massive profits over its first couple of decades. Because the corporation was so successful and outpacing the competition, its founder/CEO, board of directors, and leadership developed an attitude. They thought, "We are so successful, no one else knows more about what we do than we do. Why do we need to ask for outside opinions?" As a result, the company closed itself off to outside influences and advice. However, while the leaders were busy looking inward, the business environment was changing, and new technologies were coming to market. Many of the new technologies were from outside their industry and entered their marketspace. They had no idea how drastically the advancements would affect their industry.

---

[144] (Livingston, 2014)

The company wanted to continue to expand its reach in the marketplace and bought a tech division from a prestigious global firm. The global firm had a reputation for bringing new technologies to the market. It rarely sold any of its divisions, much less any patents, yet it initiated the sale. That should have been the first warning sign. Because the founder/CEO and his leadership were looking inward, they were unaware of emerging technologies and thought they were buying cutting-edge tech. Shortly after the purchase was final, the selling firm launched its new technologies, which made the acquired division, its tech patents, and inventory almost worthless. The company paid with cash on hand and used capital loans based on the value of the inventory and patents. Once these assets lost value, the company held hundreds of millions of dollars in unsellable inventory and meaningless patents. As a result, its stock value tanked, it was close to bankruptcy, and the shareholders, who were losing on their investments, elected new board members. The new board forced out the founder/CEO and hired a new president/CEO.

As we discussed in Chapter Seven, the new president/CEO was a progressive triple-loop thinker/leader. He wanted to change the closed-system thinking/leading (single-loop) corporate culture to open-system thinking/leading (double/triple-loop). System thinking is a way of looking at how an organization or any complex entity works. For instance, your body consists of many systems, such as pulmonary, nervous, digestive, and others. If we listen to our doctors and fitness coaches' advice, we will exercise our minds and bodies, eat healthily, and be mentally alert. Our biological and mental systems work together to keep us running efficiently and effectively. Another way to help understand system thinking might be to go to YouTube and search for "3D Movie – How a car engine works." Did you watch the short video or one you liked? An engine has many parts; each part has a role; when all the pieces are performing their tasks, they form a functioning system that transforms energy into power.

System thinking looks at the whole system, its parts, transforming functions, and outcomes, i.e., holistically. The system is the sum of its interconnected parts. If the systems' components are not maintained and updated, they become outdated, worn, and eventually irrelevant as technologies advance. System thinking is the foundation for understanding how to create business value. As a people leader, it is your role to understand the system and how those you lead fit into it and interact with each other. **System thinking empowers leaders to see the whole picture and make better decisions.**

There are two major types of organizational system thinking; open and closed. Open-system thinkers are aware of what's happening around them. Their eyes are wide open to the changes that take place in the surrounding business environment and react to changes. Closed-system thinkers are the opposite. They function in bubbles, closed off from outside considerations and influences, and therefore see no need to change. We will discuss open and closed-system thinking later in this chapter.

The new president/CEO knew, if the company was to recover and grow, it needed to embrace change and use open-system thinking. The company's closed-system thinking allowed its infrastructure to age, its teams' skillsets to become stagnant, and its processes to become inefficient, ineffective, and unproductive.

As a part of the change effort, the change team engaged human resources, corporate training, and marketing to help spread the word and motivate managers to support the change. Two of the executive teams' goals were to shift how leaders thought about people and process management and unlock the creativity and problem-solving potential of the organization's teams. I was fortunate to work with one of the new field-based national vice presidents who believed in change. Together we broke down silos between corporate headquarters and field managers and engaged his managers from first-level to top-level management. **We developed a symbiotic relationship, and in doing so, we each reached our goals.**

The recovery took three years. As a result of the changes, the company prospered. In the process, it regained many of its competitive advantages, morale increased, and customer and employee satisfaction was high. The company also paid off $800 million in debt. Considering the company was worth $1.2 billion, that is a spectacular number and means it was incredibly financially sound. Its infrastructure and communication processes also became modernized, effective, and efficient. **Teamwork, collaborative interdependency, and cooperation release effective power.** System thinking promotes these ideas.

Open Versus Closed-System Thinking

In his classic management book, "*Images of Organizations,*" Gareth Morgan, describes types of organizations through metaphors. Several of the metaphors he uses include "corporate blindness, organizational psychic prisons, and instruments of domination."[145] Corporate blindness and psychic (mental) prisons result when a company thinks of itself as a closed system. Closed systems do not consider changes in the business environment around them. We can see this effect in the manufacturing industry in America. While other nations adopted TQM, Six Sigma, and customer-centric, continuous-improvement methodologies, many industries ignored the threat of global competition. **Closed systems do not welcome input from outside resources.**

Many closed-system thinkers develop a "we know it all" attitude, and therefore do not consult those who are "lower in the ranks" or external expert resources. Closed systems produce a corporate culture and way of thinking that does not embrace the freedom of thought or novel ideas. Phrases such as "we've always done it this way" and "don't rock the boat" are typical of companies that have created psychic prisons. Mental prisons result when leaders discourage employees from being creative and looking outside the status quo for ideas. Workers and mid-level leaders become afraid to offer their opinions. Management views creativity and new ideas as a challenge to their authority, resulting in employees feeling at risk when sharing suggestions for change. When this happens, corporations and leaders can become as Morgan calls them "instruments of domination." **Open-system thinking helps prevent corporate blindness, corporate psychic prisons, and organizational leaders from becoming instruments of domination.**[146]

---

[145] (Morgan, 2006)
[146] (Morgan, 2006)

As a part of the next phase in management evolution, the differences between those who lead using closed-system versus open-system methods will become blatantly clear. The more mature you grow as a leader, the more you will view the workplace and organizations as systems. Every aspect of organizational life and business process intertwine with one another. They create a network of systems or a meta-system. A change in one system will have a reactive change in another.[147] Organizations are so much more than groups of people who complete procedures to create value from inputs and outputs. They are more than profit-making mechanisms. Corporations consist of living beings, with feelings and needs; each person has a unique reality and experiences at work. As a leader, your role is to guide them, individually, as teams, and divisions, using your distinctive skills.

Positive People Management

To shift the company's thinking on people management, we engaged human resources (HR) and corporate training to educate the leaders on the difference between Human Resource Management (HRM) and Human Capital Theory (HCT), which was what they were practicing. Why is it important to understand the difference between HRM and HCT? One imprisons individual creativity and team power, and one sets them free! **Human Resource Management creates a safe environment that empowers teamwork and unlocks creative potential.** When employees feel safe, they are not afraid to share their ideas and opinions. Whether individually or in groups, HRM uses positive psychology to encourage employees to bring their best efforts and

---

[147] (Morgan, 2006)

intentions. HRM and positive leadership psychology are proven methods to maximize organizational performance.

HCT is a traditional form of management and has not been able to resolve inequalities in the workplace. Earlier in the "We Were Cogs in a Machine" section, we talked about how it dehumanizes employees and treats them as objects from which to make a profit. HCT assumes that labor market conditions are gender-neutral, non-biased and that the matching of workers to job roles is efficient. These are faulty assumptions and perpetuate workplace inequality, such as the gender wage gap.[148] Inequalities reduce an organization's ability to meet workers' social needs, and thereby produce lower morale. Low morale can result in lower productivity, and lower productivity results in poor company performance. Many times, companies who practice HCT adopt unhealthy practices to avoid the lower productivity it produces,[149] which is what happened to the company.

Alternatives to traditional management theories began to surface in the 1950s, '60s, and '70s. Chris Argyris' organizational learning, Frederick Herzberg's motivation, and Douglas McGregor's X-Y Management theories began applying Organization Development (OD) ideas and democratic rule to the workplace. These social scientists created alternatives to bureaucratic, top-down, centralized management. It wasn't until the 1960s that Human Resource Management theory (HRM) became widely known. **HRM motivates workers by meeting their needs.** The original set

---

[148] (Huffman, 2012)
[149] (Morgan, 2006)

151

of needs was Maslow's Hierarchy of Needs; physiological, security, social, ego, and self-actualizing.[150]

Think about the timing of HRMs arrival in light of the generational shift happening in today's workforce. The older generations learned HCT. HCT creates a division of labor between management and workers. It then uses the division to justify authoritative management rule, which demoralizes workforces.[151] It squashes creativity and individualism and discourages innovation. It imprisons a workforce, does not appreciate diversity, and is single-loop, closed-system oriented.[152]

Ask yourself and other generations about these HCT characteristics:

- How does it make you feel to be treated as an object from which someone else makes a profit, i.e., produces capital?
- How does it feel to have your human needs ignored in the workplace?
- Is using money and punishment as motivators, the best way to motivate you?
- How does not being able to overcome or solve discrimination issues such as the gender wage gap and other inequalities affect your attitude and commitment to your employer?
- How do you feel when the workplace discourages you from sharing ideas, suggesting change, and taking on innovative challenges?

---

[150] (Morgan, 2006)
[151] (Bronner, 2011)
[152] (Bronner, 2011)

Write down your answers. Now compare your answers to the following reasons people and high performers typically leave jobs.

According to the Harvard Business Review, "generally people leave their jobs because they don't like their boss, don't see opportunities for promotion or growth, or are offered a better gig (and often higher pay); these reasons have held steady for years."[153] However, "it's not just what happens at work— it's what happens in someone's personal life that determines when he or she decides to look for a new job," according to Brian Kropp of CEB, Washington, D.C.[154]

The top six reasons top performers leave are:

- Tired of absorbing extra work others don't get done.
- Work is not challenging, so they disengage.
- Prevented from following new ideas and feel stifled.
- No professional development opportunities.
- Not appreciated or recognized for their work.
- Unfair compensation; includes more than money.[155]

HRM practices can help address these reasons. By nature, it is people-centered, open-system oriented, and considers external socioeconomic factors that affect meeting employees' needs. HRM-led companies, ask for external input, incorporate leading practices, and take advice from consultants and experts. They embrace innovation, change,

---

[153] (Harvard Business Review, 2016)
[154] (Harvard Business Review, 2016)
[155] (Prossack, 2018)

creativity, and listen to employee feedback. The bottom line is that **HRM is conscious of the human side of leading and does a better job of managing, motivating, developing, and retaining talent.**

Creative Problem-Solving

Creative Problem-Solving (CPS) has its roots in marketing and advertising. Alex Osborn, the founder of the Creative Education Foundation, was an advertising executive and invented creative thinking and brainstorming. In the 1920s and '30s, he and three gentlemen owned the largest advertising agency in the United States, BBDO. You might have heard of it, today it generates over $15 billion in revenue and goes by the name of the Omnicom Group of Companies.[156] CPS uses scientific research and behavioral psychology to create innovative ways to solve problems. Brainstorming was just the first. There are many augmentations and new strategies. Some I'm sure you've heard of like SWOT analysis, SMART goal creation, Blue Ocean strategies, and Mind Mapping.

A widely adopted method for high-performance team-building is the FourSight Creative method, which we mentioned earlier in Chapter Six on Transformational Leadership. IBM, NASA, USBank, L'Oréal, Nike, and other mega organizations use this method to assign roles within workgroups in a way that bolsters creativity, innovation, and project success. Its strategy identifies the way employees think and places them into four categories of thinker types; Clarifiers, Ideators, Developers, and Implementers.[157] Armed with this knowledge, leaders can intelligently assign

---

[156] (Omnicom Group, 2019)
[157] (FourSight, 2018)

roles within workgroups. **The FourSight Creative method is proving to be a game-changer in problem-solving and team performance management.**

If you want to become an expert at unlocking the creative and innovative potential of your teams, I encourage you to become certified in either CPS or the FourSight Creative method. As business schools and corporate training programs update their leadership curriculums, they cannot afford to ignore the scientifically proven strategies we've discussed. If you choose to obtain an undergraduate degree, postgraduate degree, certification, or graduate certificate in leadership, make sure to choose one that is innovation, creativity, IIRM, or OD-oriented.

Continuous Process Improvement

Take a breath and let's refocus on the example we've been discussing. The company was implementing a change initiative sponsored by the new president/CEO. The infrastructure and communication processes had become antiquated. To handle redesigning them, we engaged the new SVP of IT and SVP of supply chain. These two SVPs and I had the pleasure of introducing the company to continuous process improvement strategies from LEAN and Six Sigma methodologies. If you remember from earlier chapters, CPI began taking root in Japan in the 1940s and '50s with TQM and The Toyota Way. Since then, many other methodologies and tools have developed. The most crucial elements we used were Value Chain Analysis and Kaizen meetings. We needed to hear from those in the trenches. From those who had firsthand experience as to the effectiveness and failures of the business processes. We found out what worked, what didn't, and gathered their ideas on how to improve. I remember one process required

54 human touches to process and took as long as two weeks. That's crazy! After the process reengineering was complete, it only took seven steps and was completed in less than a day!

There are lots of cool topics; process mapping, root cause analysis, 5S model, the visual workplace with Kanbans, SIPOC, DMIAC…ok, ok, I'm geeking out. What can I say? I'm a leadership geek! Project Management is a close relative of CPI. To compare a few project management methodologies, you can check out www.lucidchart.com[158]. To learn more about CPI, invest in the book, *"Strategic Continuous Process Improvement"* by Gerhard Plenert, Ph.D.[159]

Automatic Growth

When leading a department, division, or organization, it is indispensable to combine these four tools; system thinking, positive people management, creative problem solving, and continuous process improvement. Tie them together with an organizational design that strategically focuses on leadership agreement, interdependency, interactive and lateral communications, collaboration, and cooperation. In doing so, leaders can structure functional and people systems to automatically encourage behaviors that drive their desired business outcomes. Once the systems are running, less time and effort is needed to manage repeatable tasks, allowing more time to explore fresh, innovative ways to grow.

Innovative leaders use autopoietic systems to automate people and functional activities. Building a reward system

---

[158] (Lucidchart, 2017)
[159] (Plenert, 2012)

that includes interdependent goals, by design, permeates the organization's culture with agreement and cooperation. The interdependent goals tie people and business outcomes from multiple systems together. Collaborative teamwork, cooperation, and agreement with corporate directives are built into the system structures. Everyone benefits when all people and systems are pulling in the same direction. It is the fulfillment of the old saying, "one for all, and all for one."

Although I would like nothing more than to dive further into automated growth, it encompasses a deep understanding of meta-systems and complex adaptive systems, and that stretches far beyond the bounds of this book. However, I hope to have the opportunity to discuss how to create autopoietic systems that perpetuate vitality and organizational growth with you in person. I look forward to meeting you, whether on a leadership webinar, as a member in my private mentorship group, or at a sponsored leadership event by your organization.

Thanks for your desire to be the best leader you can be. I'm sure your future will be bright as you develop and mature as a leader. As you choose to lead, don't go at it alone, reach out for assistance. All great leaders have a mentor or coach; I've had many and still do. Now, there are just a few things left as we wrap up our journey through this book.

Reflections

Take five minutes and reflect on what you've learned. Write down at least three takeaways. At the end of the book you will have 30+ key ideas to review that will help mold your thinking, build bridges, and bolster your leadership skills.

1._____

_____

_____

_____

_____

2._____

_____

_____

_____

_____

3._____

_____

_____

_____

_____

_____

_____

_____

_____

Chapter 11: Your Future in Leadership

In the coming years, many of the leadership terms we have discussed will be at the forefront of leadership development and coaching. The most considerable leadership challenge facing our nation, and the world, is how to lead teams and organizations through the next phase of democratic organizational leadership. **The resources we have covered will help you grow as a leader and avoid becoming a "dead leader walking."** The deeper you dig in each area we've discussed, the more self-discovery you will experience. Becoming self-aware is a part of every great leader's journey.[160]

Choosing to Lead

One of the most important ideas in leadership development is the concept of "use of self." The idea is that *you* are an indispensable tool in your leadership toolbox.[161] **Developing yourself mentally, emotionally, physically, and spiritually is a crucial step in becoming a great leader.** There are many specialty disciplines within the realm of leadership. Use the advice given in the section, "Value of Career Choice," and choose an area that fills you with passion. Then go for it!

Reflections & Personal Leadership Development Plan

The word for today is "now". It is time for you to act! Use the following pages to create your personal leadership action plan. You are destined for greatness. Choose to lead positively!

---

[160] (Jones & Brazzel, 2014)
[161] (Jones & Brazzel, 2014)

1. Reflect on your key moments and thoughts from reading this book.
2. Rewrite your key takeaways from each chapter.
3. Reread them. Which ones stand out the most?
4. Write YOUR personal mission and vision statement for the type of leader that you want to be or become.
5. List the areas that you MUST GROW in.
6. This is your personal action plan. Embrace it, follow it, and be the great leader I know you are destined to become!

Key Reflections

1._____
_____
_____
_____
_____
_____

2._____
_____
_____
_____
_____
_____

3._____
_____
_____
_____
_____
_____

4.

5.

6.

7.

8.

9._____

10._____

11._____

12._____

13._____

14._____

15._____

16._____

17._____

18.

19.

20.

21.

22.

23.

24.

25.

26.

27.

28._____

29._____

30._____

Write your personal leadership mission/vision statement for a more brilliant you. What do you want your life to look like in five years?

1._____

2._____
_____
_____
_____
_____
_____

3._____
_____
_____
_____
_____
_____

What steps must you take NOW to make your future
come to pass?

1._____
_____
_____
_____
_____

I commit to completing by (date):_____
2._____
_____
_____
_____

I commit to completing by (date):_____

3._____

_____

_____

_____

_____

I commit to completing by (date):_____

4._____

_____

_____

_____

_____

I commit to completing by (date):_____

5._____

_____

_____

_____

_____

I commit to completing by (date):_____

I _____, choose to be
the best leader I can be. I choose to lead positively, and be
an overcomer, sincere communicator, relationship builder,
creative innovator, team builder, bridge-building, chasm-
crossing, gap-filling, emotionally and culturally woke
motivational leader.

Signature: _____

Date:_____

Chapter 12: Your Invitation

Joining a community of peers for support, inspiration, collaboration, and advice is one of the most vital actions you will ever take in becoming a great leader and succeeding at work and life. None of us are as smart as all of us, and leadership development groups of like-minded people are a powerful way to cultivate community. We need leaders who want to lead us to a future where people are respected, and all four G's of growth become a reality; consistent growth, competitive growth, profitable growth, and responsible growth. We need to go beyond talk, and act.

I invite you to learn and to lead well. Going at it alone is one of the toughest routes anyone can take, and few succeed without training and coaching. Nothing great happens without a team. If you would like someone to come along side and support you through your journey, someone who is genuinely interested and cares about seeing you succeed, call me. The first hour's one me, let's talk.
www.ithinkyouthink.com

You can do it! You can positively change your world.

Coach Buschman, Ph.D.(c)

References

Amabile, T., & Kramer, S. (2011). *The Progress Principle.* Boston, MA: Harvard Business Review Press.

Ambedkar, B. R. (1936, 1937, 1944, 2018). *Annihilation of Caste.* New Delhi, India: Rupa Publications.

America Counts Staff. (2019, February 21). *Education.* Retrieved from United States Census Bureau: https://www.census.gov/library/stories/2019/02/number-of-people-with-masters-and-phd-degrees-double-since-2000.html

Apple. (1984). *Apple 1984 Commercial.* Retrieved from YouTube: https://www.youtube.com/results?search_query=Apple+1984+Commercial

Associated Press. (2008, September 18). *In Hard Times, Tent Cities Rise Up Across the Country.* Retrieved from Life on NBC NEWS: http://www.nbcnews.com/id/26776283/ns/us_news-life/t/hard-times-tent-cities-rise-across-country/#.XIqSxNF7l0s

Associated Press. (2015, July 9). *Actor Tom Selleck Reaches Tentative Settlement with Water District.* Retrieved from CBS NEWS: https://www.cbsnews.com/news/actor-tom-selleck-reaches-tentative-settlement-with-water-district/

Barton, C. (2013, March 18). *Traveling with Millennials.* Retrieved from Boston Consulting Group: https://www.bcg.com/publications/2013/transportation-tourism-marketing-sales-traveling-millennials.aspx

Bartz, C. (2009, November 13). *Leadership in the information age.* Retrieved September 3, 2017, from

The Economist:
http://www.economist.com/node/14742618

BCorporation. (2019). *A Global Community of Leaders.*
Retrieved from BCorporation:
https://bcorporation.net/?gclid=EAIaIQobChMIlq
6R8Y3R5AIVhMDICh2msQ1XEAAYASAAEgL9-
_D_BwE

Bernhard, B. (2018, June 18). *St. Louis Post-Dispatch.*
Retrieved from Federal report: Coldwater Creek
Contamination May Raise the Risk of Cancer in
North St. Louis County Residents:
https://www.stltoday.com/news/local/metro/fed
eral-report-coldwater-creek-contamination-may-
raise-the-risk-of/article_b70fd34c-c07d-5cee-8348-
f76d3d4a90eb.html

Blake, R., & McCanse, A. (1991). *Leadership Dilemmas-
Grid® Solutions.* Houston, TX: Gulf Professional
Publishing.

Bogdan, C. (2016, December 12). *One in 6 Americans Take
Antidepressants, Other Psychiatric Drugs: Study.*
Retrieved from NBC NEWS:
https://www.nbcnews.com/health/health-
news/one-6-americans-take-antidepressants-other-
psychiatric-drugs-n695141

Borge, J. (2019, April 12). *Here's What All of Those Popular
Slang Words Really Mean.* Retrieved from The
Oprah Magazine:
https://www.oprahmag.com/entertainment/g236
03568/slang-words-meaning/?slide=12

Bozzo, S., & McDowel, M. (2008). *Blue Water Wars.*
Retrieved from Shop PBS:
https://shop.pbs.org/blue-gold-world-water-wars-
dvd/product/BGWW601?productId=3477137

Bronner, S. (2011). *Critical Theory: A Very Short Introduction*. Oxford, UK: Oxford University Press.

Brown, J., Homer, K., & Isaacs, D. (2007). The World Cafe'. In P. Holman, T. Devane, & S. Cady, *Change Handbook: The Definitive Resource on Today's Best Methods for Engaging Whole Systems* (pp. pgs. 73-88). San Francisco, CA: Berrett-Koehler Publishers, Inc.

Burnes, B. (2006). Kurt Lewin and the Planned Approach to Change. In J. Gallos, *Organization Development* (pp. pp. 133 - 157). San Francisco, CA: Josey-Bass.

Buschman, L. (2017, December 21). Leadership and the Golden Rule. (G. Buschman, Interviewer)

Cartwright, S. (2002). Double-Loop Learning: A Concept and Process for Leadership Educators. . *Journal of Leadership Education*, Vol. 1, Issue 1, Pgs. 68-71.

CelebrityTV. (2019, April 8). *UPDATE: Auburn Star Gymnast Retires After Breaking Legs During Competition [GRAPHIC PICS]*. Retrieved from YouTube: https://www.youtube.com/watch?v=IlOhwsqoQB8

Center for Servant Based Leadership. (2016). *The Servant As Leader*. Retrieved from Robert K. Greenleaf Center for Servant Based Leadership: www.greenleaf.org

Center for Servant Leadership. (2016). *The Journey Starts Here*. Retrieved from Robert K. Greenleaf: Center for Servant Leadership: https://www.greenleaf.org/

Conscious Capitalism. (2019). *Welcome to Conscious Capitalism*. Retrieved from Conscious Capitalism: https://www.consciouscapitalism.org/

Cooperrider, D., & Whitney, D. (2007). Appreciative Inquiry A Positive Revolution in Change. In P. Holman, T. Devane, & S. Cady, *The Change Handbook: The Definitive Resource on Today's Best Methods for Engaging Whole Systems* (pp. pp. 74-88). San Francisco, CA: Berrett-Koehler Publishers, Inc.

Cornell University. (2019). *Servant Leadership Certificate from Cornell University.* Retrieved from eCornell: https://info.ecornell.com/servant-leadership

Costanza, D., Badger, J., Fraser, R., Severt, J., & Gade, P. (2012). Generational Differences in Work-Related Attitudes: A Meta-analysis. *Journal of Business and Psychology*, Vol. 24, No.2, pp. 375-394.

Craver, J. (2019, August 5). *Gen X: The 'Forgotten Generation' Gets Overlooked for Workplace Promotions.* Retrieved from Credit Union Times: https://www.cutimes.com/2019/08/05/gen-x-the-forgotten-generation-gets-overlooked-for-workplace-promotions-413-160525/?slreturn=20191118112050

Creative Commons License. (2009, April 22). *From a Movie to a Movement.* Retrieved from Te Story of Stuff: https://storyofstuff.org/

Daniels, M. D., & Price, P. V. (2009). *The Essential Enneagram.* New York, NY: HarperCollins.

Davy, K., & Harris PhD, S. (2005). *Value Redesigned: New Models For Professional Practice.* Atlanta, GA: Greenway Communications, LLC.

Dewey, J. (1916, 1944, 1997). *Democracy and Education.* New York, NY: The Free Press.

Dimock, M. (2019, January 17). *Fact Tank: News in the Numbers.* Retrieved from Pew Research Center: https://www.pewresearch.org/fact-tank/2019/01/17/where-millennials-end-and-generation-z-begins/

eCoast. (2018, August 11). *Remembering the Tsunami of August 1868*. Retrieved from eCoast: https://www.ecoast.co.nz/tsunami-of-august-1868/

Eisenberg, R. (2019, March 25). *Gen X: Least Happy At Work, Most Financially Stressed*. Retrieved from Forbes: https://www.forbes.com/sites/nextavenue/2019/03/25/gen-x-least-happy-at-work-most-financially-stressed/#22827c66b747

Forster, M. (Director). (2008). *Quantum of Solace* [Motion Picture].

Forsyth, D. (1980). A Taxonomy of Ethical Ideologies. *Journal of Personality and Social Psychology*, Vol. 30, pp. 175-184.

FourSight. (2018, January 28). *FourSight Home*. Retrieved from FourSight: www.foursightonline.com/

Fry, R. (2018, April 11). *Millennials are the Largest Generation in the U.S. Labor Force*. Retrieved from Pew Research Center - FactTank News in the Numbers: http://www.pewresearch.org/fact-tank/2014/06/05/generation-x-americas-neglected-middle-child/

Galbraith, J., Downey, D., & Kates, A. (2001). *Designing Dynamic Organizations*. New York, NY: AMACOM. Retrieved from Galbraith Management Consultants, LTD.: https://www.jaygalbraith.com/services/star-model

Gallup. (2017). *State Of The American Workplace*. Retrieved from Gallup:

https://www.gallup.com/workplace/238085/state
-american-workplace-report-2017.aspx

Green, D. D., & Roberts, G. E. (2012). Impact of
Postmodernism on Public Sector Leadership
Practices: Federal Government Human Capital
Development Implications . *Sage: Public Personnel
Management,* 79-96.

Gregory, J. (2009). *The Great Depression in Washington
State* . Retrieved from Hoovervilles and
Homelessness:
http://depts.washington.edu/depress/hooverville.
shtml

Harvard Business Review. (2016). Why People Quit Their
Jobs. *Harvard Business Review,* pp. 20-21.

Hershatter, A., & Epstein, M. (2010). Millennials and the
World of Work: An Organization and Management
Perspective. *Journal of Business and Psychology,*
Vol. 25, No. 2, pp. 211-223.

Hill, C. (2019, March 26). *The Quiet Desperation of Gen X
Workers Across America* . Retrieved from MSN
MarketWatch: https://www.msn.com/en-
us/money/careersandeducation/the-quiet-
desperation-of-gen-x-workers-across-america/ar-
BBVbRlI?ocid=se

Hinote, S. C., & Sundvall, T. J. (2015). Leading Millennials.
Air & Space Power Journal, pp. 131-138.

Holland, K. (2015, February 4). *Fighting With Your Spouse?
It's Probably About This.* Retrieved from
www.cnbc.com:
https://www.cnbc.com/2015/02/04/money-is-
the-leading-cause-of-stress-in-relationships.html

Huffman, M. (2012). Organizations, Managers, and Wage
Inequality. *Sex Roles,* Pgs, 216-222.

Hughes, R., & Ginnett, R. &. (2015). *Leadership: Enhancing the Lessons of Experience.* New York, New York: McGraw-Hill.

Inamori, K. (2013). *Amoeba Management: The Dynamic Management System for Rapid Market Response 1st Edition* . Boca Raton, FL: CRC Press.

Jiang, J. (2018, May 2). *Millennials Stand Out for Their Technology Use, but Older Generations also Embrace Digital Life.* Retrieved from Pew Research Center: Fact Tank News in the Numbers: https://www.pewresearch.org/fact-tank/2018/05/02/millennials-stand-out-for-their-technology-use-but-older-generations-also-embrace-digital-life/

Johnson, D., & Johnson, F. (2013). *Joining Together: Group Theory and Group Skills.* Upper Saddle River, NJ: Pearson.

Jones, B., & Brazzel, M. (2014). *The NTL Handbook of Organization Development and Change: Principles, Practices, and Perspectives.* San Francisco, CA: Wiley.

Kapoor, C., & Solomon, N. (2011). Understanding and managing generational differences in the workplace. . *Worldwide Hospitality and Tourism Themes*, 308-318.

KickMari Sports. (2016, August 6). *Rio Olympics French gymnast breaks a leg on landing.* Retrieved from YouTube: https://www.youtube.com/watch?v=8qBmUVVkBjw

Kouzes, J., & Posner, B. (2017). *The Leadership Challenge Sixth Edition.* Hoboken, NJ: John Wiley & Sons, Inc.

Langer, E. (2016, June 9). *Psychology Today.* Retrieved from Self-Esteem vs. Self-Respect: https://www.psychologytoday.com/us/articles/19 9911/self-esteem-vs-self-respect

Lebow, V. (1955). Price Competition in 1955. *Journal of Retailing.*

Livingston, R. (2014). The Future of Organization Development in a VUCA World. In B. Jones, & M. Brazzel, *The NTL Handbook of Organization Development and Change: Principles, Practices, and Perspectives* (pp. pgs. 659-673). New York, NY: Center for Creative Leadership.

Lucidchart. (2017, October 23). *Agile vs. Waterfall vs. Kanban vs. Scrum: What's the Difference?* Retrieved from Lucidchart: https://www.lucidchart.com/blog/agile-vs-waterfall-vs-kanban-vs-scrum

Manwani, H. (2013, October). *Ideas Worth Spreading.* Retrieved from TED: https://www.ted.com/talks/harish_manwani_prof it_s_not_always_the_point?language=en

Maxwell, J. (2013). *The Seventeen Irrefutable Laws of Teamwork: Embrace Them and Empower Your Team.* New York, NY: HarperCollins.

McCormick, J. (2018). *The First-Time Manager.* New York, NY: HarperCollins Leadership.

McCoy, D. (2010). *Leadership Building Blocks: An Insider's Guide to Success.* Sacramento, CA: Flourish Publishing Group.

Merriam-Webster. (n.d.). *Definition of Reckless.* Retrieved from Merriam-Webster: https://www.merriam-webster.com/dictionary/reckless

Metcalf, M., & Palmer, M. (2011). *Innovative Leadership Fieldbook.* Tucson, AZ: Integral Publishers.

Mill, J. S. (2002). *On Liberty: John Stuart Mill.* Mineola, NY: Dover Publications, Inc.

Mind Tools. (n.d.). *The Blake Mouton Managerial Grid Leading: People and Producing Results* . Retrieved from Mind Tools: https://www.mindtools.com/pages/article/newLDR_73.htm

Morgan, G. (2006). *Images of Organizations.* Thousand Oaks, CA: Sage Publications.

Mya, K. (2017, February 3). *Why Millennials Have Become the Wanderlust Generation.* Retrieved from UsNews: https://travel.usnews.com/features/why-millennials-have-become-the-wanderlust-generation

Myers, K., & Sadaghiani, K. (2010). Millennials in the Workplace: A Communication Perspective on Millennials' Organizational Relationships and Performance. *Journal of Business and Psychology,* Vol. 25, No. 2, pp.225-238.

Omnicom Group. (2019, October 10). *News, Events & Filings.* Retrieved from Omnicom Group: http://investor.omnicomgroup.com/investor-relations/news-events-and-filings/default.aspx#QuarterlyEarnings

Online Etymology Dictionary. (2019). *Online Etymology Dictionary.* Retrieved from Eymonline: https://www.etymonline.com

Pearce, W. B. (2007). *The Making of Our Social Worlds: A Communication Perspective.* Malden, MA: Blackwell Publishing.

Phillips, C. (2011, March 16). *The 10 Most Destructive Tsunamis in History.* Retrieved from Australian Geographic:

https://www.australiangeographic.com.au/topics/science-environment/2011/03/the-10-most-destructive-tsunamis-in-history/

Plenert, G. (2012). *Strategic Continuous Process Improvement.* New York, NY: McGraw-Hill Companies, Inc.

Prichard, S. (2013, January 24). *9 Qualities of the Servant Leader.* Retrieved from Skip Prichard Leadership Insights: https://www.skipprichard.com/9-qualities-of-the-servant-leader/

Prossack, A. (2018, November 30). *6 Reasons Your Best Employees Quit.* Retrieved from Forbes: https://www.forbes.com/sites/ashiraprossack1/2018/11/30/6-reasons-your-best-employees-quit/#126296ff2d74

Public Service Announcement. (1973). *Keep America Beautiful 1973.* Retrieved from YouTube: https://www.youtube.com/results?search_query=keep+america+beautiful+1973

Pynes, J. E. (2013). *Human Resource Management For Public and Nonprofit Organizations: A Strategic Approach (4th ed.).* San Francisco, CA: Jossey-Bass.

Real, K., Mitnick, A., & Maloney, W. (2010). More Similar than Different: Millennials in the U.S. Building Trades. *Journal of Business and Psychology,* Vol. 25, No. 2, 303-313.

Ross, D. (2009). *Aristotle: The Nicomachean Ethics.* Oxford, UK: Oxford University Press.

Schaeffer, B. (2018, December 01). *Machiavellian Leadership: How Toxicity Can Lead to an Organization's Demise.* Retrieved from FireHouse: https://www.firehouse.com/leadership/article/21025131/machiavellian-leadership-how-toxicity-can-lead-to-an-organizations-demise

Seidi, D. (2004). *Munich School of Business.* Retrieved from LMU: Ludwig-Maximilians Universität Munchen: https://www.zfog.bwl.uni-muenchen.de/files/mitarbeiter/paper2004_2.pdf

Sessa, V. I., Kabacoff, R. I., Deal, J., & Brown, H. (2007). Generational Differences in Leader Values and Leadership Behaviors. . *The Psychologist-Manager Journal,* 47-74.

Slater, R. (1999). *Jack Welch and the GE Way.* New York, New York: McGraw-Hill.

Smith, A. (1776). *The Wealth of Nations.*

Sorenson, S., & Garman, K. (2013, June 11). *How to Tackle U.S. Employees' Stagnating Engagement.* Retrieved from GALLUP NEWS: https://news.gallup.com/businessjournal/162953/tackle-employees-stagnating-engagement.aspx

Stack Exchange. (n.d.). *English Language & Usage.* Retrieved from Stack Exchange: https://english.stackexchange.com/questions/349045/the-origin-of-the-word-aw-shucks

Taylor, P., & Gao, G. (2014, June 5). *Generation X: America's neglected 'middle child'.* Retrieved September 2, 2017, from PEW Research Center: http://www.pewresearch.org/fact-tank/2014/06/05/generation-x-americas-neglected-middle-child/

The World Cafe'. (2019). *The World Cafe'.* Retrieved from http://www.theworldcafe.com

The World Cafe. (2019). *The World Cafe: Shaping Our Futures Through Conversations That Matter.* Retrieved from The World Cafe: http://www.theworldcafe.com/

Tony Robbins. (2019). *Find Your True Self*. Retrieved from
Tony Robbins:
https://www.tonyrobbins.com/disc/.

Torbert, B. (2004). *Action Inquiry: The Secret of Timely
and Transforming Leadership*. San Francisco:
Berrett-Koehler Publishers, Inc.

Tosey, P., Visser, M., & Saunders, M. (2011, December 2).
*The origins and conceptualizations of 'triple-loop'
learning: A critical review*. Retrieved from Sage
Journals: Management Learning:
epubs.surrey.ac.uk/7446/8/Tosey_The_origins_an
d_conceptualisations.pdf

Toyota, Inc. (2012). *75 Years of Toyota, Even Better Cars*.
Retrieved from Toyota-Global:
https://www.toyota-
global.com/company/history_of_toyota/75years/
data/conditions/philosophy/toyotaway2001.html

U.S. Bureau of Labor Statistics. (2015, December). *United
States Department of Labor*. Retrieved from U.S.
Bureau of Labor Statistics:
https://www.bls.gov/opub/mlr/2015/article/labo
r-force-projections-to-2024.htm

U.S. Bureau of Labor Statistics. (2019). *Employment
Projections - 2018-2028, USDL-19-1571*.
Washington, D.C.: U.S.. Department of Labour.

Unilever. (2019). *Sustainable Living*. Retrieved from
Unilever: https://www.unilever.com/sustainable-
living/

Unilever PLC. (2005, October 02). *Unilever Streamlines Its
Leadership Structure*. Retrieved from Unilever:
https://www.unilever.com/news/press-
releases/2005/05-02-10-Unilever-streamlines-its-
leadership-structure.html

VanMeter, R., Grisaffe, D., Chonko, L., & Roberts, J. (2013). Generation Y's Ethical Ideology and Its Potential Workplace Implications. *Journal of Business Ethics*, Vol. 117, No. 1, pp. 93-109.

Waldek, S. (2018, January 22). *8 Multi-Million-Dollar Masterpieces Found in Unexpected Places*. Retrieved from History: https://www.history.com/news/8-multi-million-dollar-masterpieces-found-in-unexpected-places

Welch, J., & Byrne, J. (2009). *Jack: Straight from the Gut*. New York, New York: Werner Books.

Zemke, R., Raines, C., & Filipczak, B. (2013). *Generations at Work: Managing the Clash of Boomers, Gen Xers, and Gen Yers in the Workplace*. New York, New York: American Management Association.

Zigarelli, M. (2013, August 17). *Ten Leadership Theories in Five Minutes*. Retrieved from YouTube: https://www.youtube.com/watch?v=XKUPDUD OBVo&feature=youtu.be

About Greg Buschman, Ph.D.(c)

 I am a husband and father of four young adults. As you will see on my personal webpage and on Facebook, my family and I love to travel. We enjoy spending family time together exploring different cultures and their histories. www.gregbuschman.us.

I started in business as an entrepreneur and learned to squeeze 60 hours of work into 40 hours (*or less*). Effective efficiency served me well, and in my first corporate role, I made rookie of the year by revitalizing an underperforming territory. As a regional/national leader, I transformed underperforming teams, departments, and divisions into high performers. As measured by industry averages, my areas of responsibility produced millions of dollars in incremental growth, outpaced industry averages, and received national and global recognition. Today, I'm finishing my behavioral sciences doctorate in leadership and organizational development in "Creative Leadership for Innovation and Change." I hold master's degrees in IT and marketing management; MSIS and MSMKT.

Who I help:
I help current and emerging leaders and their organizations improve performance. I use strategies proven in my career as a top-performing leader, and those used by the world's most successful organizations. Although I cannot make any claims of an increase in your income or business outcomes, I do believe I may be able to help you be more successful and achieve better results.

How I help:
I coach leaders and organizations on how to unlock their leadership potential and the power of the multi-generational/multi-cultural workforce. I lead them through a series of step-by-step leadership development strategies. The focus is on producing positive people behaviors, positive work environments, and positive business outcomes. Following these proven strategies, leaders are better able to guide teams to meet or exceed expectations while improving their work-life experiences.

Expertise:
Multi-generational & Multi-cultural Leadership | Speaking | Advising | Leadership Coaching | Change Management | Organizational Development | Revitalization | Education

Greg can be reached at:
Email: Gregory.Buschman@gmail.com
Phone: 727-742-5045
Website: www.gregbuschman.com
Twitter: gbuschman1
Instagram: gbuschman
LinkedIn: www.linkedin.com/in/gregbuschman/
Facebook: www.facebook.com/WeAllThinkDifferently

One Last Note...

If you found the book useful and enjoyed the read, I would be appreciative if you would write a review on Amazon and our other resellers. I read these personally so that I can improve my writing skills and future books. It also helps others find the book and spread the news about positive people management and how they might have a better future.

You can always send a review and your thoughts directly to me at www.gregbuschman.com/contact.

Thanks for helping!!

PS Don't forget to your complimentary gift:
www.ithinkyouthink.com/freecallorwebinar

Made in United States
Orlando, FL
18 January 2022

13714414R00104